# PLASTIC CANVAS
# Stitch by Stitch™

Edited by Vicki Blizzard

the Needlecraft Shop

| | |
|---:|:---|
| Editor | VICKI BLIZZARD |
| Managing Editor | KELLY KEIM |
| Associate Editor | TANYA TURNER |
| Technical Editor | JUNE SPRUNGER |
| Copy Editors | MICHELLE BECK |
| | MARY MARTIN |
| Book Design | ERIN AUGSBERGER |
| Cover Design | GREG SMITH |
| Production Artist | DEBBY KEEL |
| Photography Supervisor | SCOTT CAMPBELL |
| Photographer | ANDY J. BURNFIELD |
| Photo Department Assistants | MARTHA COQUAT |
| | CRYSTAL KEY |
| Chief Executive Officer | JOHN ROBINSON |
| Publishing Director | DAVID MCKEE |
| Book Marketing Director | CRAIG SCOTT |
| Editorial Director | VIVIAN ROTHE |
| Publishing Services Managers | BRENDA GALLMEYER |
| | ANGE VAN ARMAN |
| Customer Service | (800) 449-0440 |
| Pattern Services | (903) 636-5140 |

Library of Congress Cataloging-in-Publication Data
ISBN: 1-57367-128-2
First Printing: 2003
Library of Congress Catalog Card Number: 2002112903
Printed in the United States of America.

Visit us at
NeedlecraftShop.com

Every effort has been made to ensure the accuracy and completeness of the
instructions in this book. However, we cannot be responsible for human
error or for the results when using materials other than those specified in
the instructions, or for variations in individual work.

# A Note
## From the Editor

Dear Crafters,

When I was a teenager, my family moved into a new neighborhood and my mom joined a homemakers' club. One month, the club program consisted of one of the members teaching how to do a needlepoint sampler. My mom had a hard time learning the stitches, so she just brought the project home and put it in a closet.

A few months later, while on summer vacation, I was looking for something to do and pulled out that bag of canvas and yarn. I was immediately intrigued by the textures and patterns created by the sampler—it was like creating magic with a needle and yarn! When my mom came home from work that afternoon, she sat with me while I taught her how to work each stitch. My mom passed away quite a few years ago, and I've long since lost track of what happened to that needlepoint sampler, but the love of teaching someone how to stitch has stayed with me all this time.

When I was planning this book, I wanted it to be like having a friend sitting next to you, patiently showing where to place your needle for each stitch to create magic patterns with your yarn. I think our group of talented designers has accomplished just this, and I hope you'll enjoy learning new stitches and creating magic projects of your own!

Warm regards,

Vicki Blizzard

# CONTENTS

## CHAPTER ONE
# Continental Stitch

## CHAPTER TWO
# Gobelin Stitch

## CHAPTER FIVE
# Cross Stitch

## CHAPTER SIX
# Square Stitch

## CHAPTER FOUR
# Long Stitch

## CHAPTER SEVEN
# Surface Embellishments

## CHAPTER EIGHT
# Fancy Joining Stitches

# CHAPTER ONE

# Continental Stitch

You can create wonderful works of art, using only the simplest of stitches!

Our Continental Stitch collection includes fabulous projects for every

**Continental Stitch**

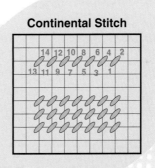

season, ranging from fanciful to festive, whimsical to elegant—every one of them makes a perfect showcase for the endlessly varied possibilities of this basic stitch!

# Leaf Study Coasters

Designs by Kathy Wirth

These **intricately detailed leaves** look
real enough to rustle up a summer breeze inside your home!

## Skill Level • Beginner

### Finished Size

5 inches square

### Materials

- 2 sheets stiff 7-count plastic canvas
- Coats & Clark Red Heart Classic worsted weight yarn Art. E267 as listed in color key
- #16 tapestry needle
- 11-inch-square sheet or roll of thin cork
- 18 inches ³/₁₆-inch plum cord
- 2 (25mm x 9mm) large-hole silver ridged cylinder beads from The Beadery
- Heavy books or other heavy objects
- Transparent cellophane tape
- Hot-glue gun

### Instructions

**1** Cut plastic canvas according to graphs. Coaster backs will remain unstitched.

**2** Stitch coaster fronts following graph, working uncoded border, highlighted in blue, with off-white Continental Stitches and uncoded areas on leaves with light sage Continental Stitches.

**3** Using one unstitched back as a template, trace four liners on cork sheet, then cut cork ¹/₁₆-inch inside traced lines, making sure to cut out inside edges.

**4** For each coaster, match edges of back and front, then Whipstitch inside edges together with cornmeal and outside edges together with dark plum.

**5** Glue cork liners to coaster backs. Place heavy books or objects on top until glue dries.

**6** Wrap transparent tape tightly around cord ends to prevent raveling. Twist each cord end through one hole of a bead. Dab glue on cord at other end of bead to secure. Insert cord through holes in coasters and tie. #

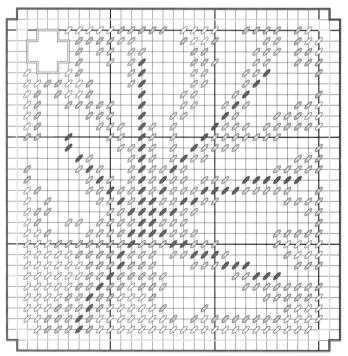

**Leaf A**
32 holes x 32 holes
Cut 2, stitch 1

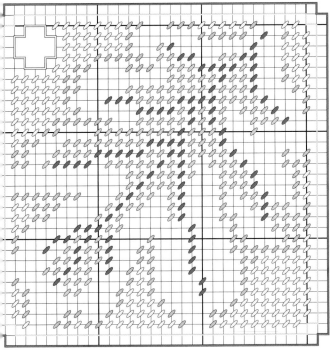

**Leaf B**
32 holes x 32 holes
Cut 2, stitch 1

| COLOR KEY | |
|---|---|
| **Worsted Weight Yarn** | **Yards** |
| ☐ Cornmeal #220 | 15 |
| ☐ Medium sage #632 | 14 |
| ■ Dark sage #633 | 8 |
| ☐ Honey gold #645 | 11 |
|   Uncoded borders (highlighted blue) | |
|   are off-white #3 Continental Stitches | 9 |
|   Uncoded areas on leaves are light | |
|   sage #631 Continental Stitches | 20 |
| ╱ Dark plum #533 Whipstitching | 9 |
| Color numbers given are for Coats & Clark Red Heart Classic worsted weight yarn Art. E267. | |

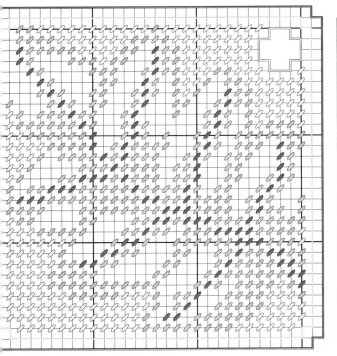

**Leaf C**
32 holes x 32 holes
Cut 2, stitch 1

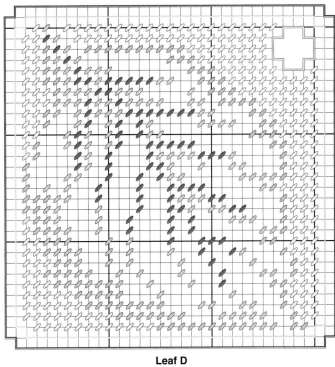

**Leaf D**
32 holes x 32 holes
Cut 2, stitch 1

# Frisky Felines Tissue Box Cover

Design by Kathy Wirth

This delightful clan of **curious kitties** brings
colorful fun to your child's playroom!

## Skill Level • Beginner

### Finished Size

Fits boutique-style tissue box

## Materials

- 1½ sheets stiff 7-count plastic canvas
- Uniek Needloft plastic canvas yarn as listed in color key
- 6-strand embroidery floss as listed in color key
- Kreinik Heavy (#32) Braid as listed in color key
- #16 tapestry needle
- #20 tapestry needle

## Instructions

**1** Cut plastic canvas according to graphs.

**2** Stitch pieces following graphs, working uncoded areas with bright purple Continental Stitches.

**3** When background stitching is completed, work black floss French Knots for eyes. For each yarn ball, use 2 strands black braid to work four Cross Stitches (Fig. 1).

**4** Use 1 strand braid to loosely work yarn string on each side where indicated, coming up at 1 and down at 2; up at 3, down at 4. Continue in this manner through 14, referring to photo to adjust curves of stitches.

**5** With another length of braid, tack loose stitches with couching stitches where indicated as follows: two times between 1 and 2, 3 and 4, and 9 and 10; and one time between 13 and 14. There are no couching stitches between 5 and 6, 7 and 8, and 11 and 12.

**6** Using black yarn throughout, Overcast inside edges of top and bottom edges of sides. Whipstitch sides together, then Whipstitch sides to top. #

| COLOR KEY | |
|---|---|
| **Plastic Canvas Yarn** | **Yards** |
| ■ Black #00 | 26 |
| ■ Fern #23 | 6 |
| □ White #41 | 18 |
| ■ Bright orange #58 | 11 |
| ■ Bright blue #60 | 7 |
| ■ Bright pink #62 | 12 |
| □ Bright yellow #63 | 12 |
| Uncoded areas are bright purple #64 Continental Stiches | 13 |
| **6-Strand Embroidery Floss** | |
| ● Black French Knot | 2 |
| **Heavy (#32) Braid** | |
| ✎ Black #005HL Quadruple Cross Stitch | 7 |
| ✎ Couch placement | |
| Color numbers given are for Uniek Needloft plastic canvas yarn and Kreinik Heavy (#32) Braid. | |

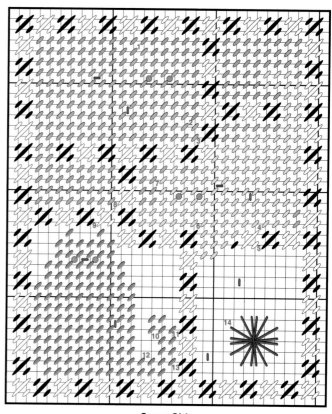

**Cover Side**
31 holes x 37 holes
Cut 4

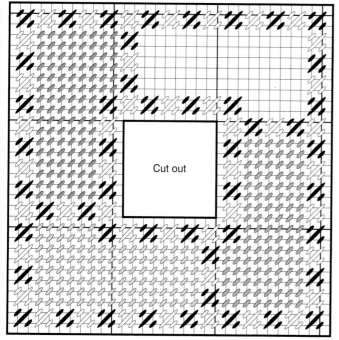

**Cover Top**
31 holes x 31 holes
Cut 1

**Fig. 1**

# Keepsake Egg

Design by Janna Britton

Brighten your home with this beautiful ornament, **lovely and fresh** as a warm spring morning!

## Skill Level • Intermediate

### Finished Size

2½ inches W x 3½ inches H

## Materials

- Small amount 10-count plastic canvas
- DMC #3 pearl cotton: 12 inches white and as listed in color key
- DMC 6-strand rayon embroidery floss as listed in color key
- DMC 6-strand cotton embroidery floss as listed in color key
- 4mm Bucilla silk ribbon as listed in color key
- #22 tapestry needle
- Small bunny brass charm #9372 by Creative Beginnings
- Clear acrylic spray sealer
- 3-inch x 4-inch piece adhesive-backed white felt from Kunin

## Cutting & Stitching

**1** Cut plastic canvas according to graph (page 15).

**2** Following graph through step 8, at top of egg, work medium pink rayon floss stitches using 6 plies, then work French Knots with 6 plies pale yellow cotton floss.

**3** Work Cross Stitches next with 3 plies each snow white and violet rayon floss.

**4** Using #3 pearl cotton, work sky with ultra very light blue and grass with forest green.

**5** Using 12 plies cotton floss throughout, Continental Stitch uncoded areas in sky and under grass with white, then work bottom part of egg with light coral and pale yellow.

**6** Work light emerald ribbon Straight Stitches for leaves. For flowers, work French Knots with 3 plies violet rayon floss and pale yellow cotton floss.

**7** Using 3 plies cotton floss, work letters using Backstitches and French Knots.

**8** Overcast edges with 12 plies white cotton floss.

## Finishing

**1** Spray bunny charm with sealer. Allow to dry. Using very light blue cotton floss, center and tack to egg so that bottom of bunny sits on top of grass.

**2** For hanger, thread ends of white pearl cotton from back to front through top center hole of egg. Keeping ends even, pull through to center of length; tie in a bow on front and trim ends as desired.

**3** Cut felt to fit egg, then apply to backside. #

# Soup-er Day Recipe Sign

Design by Celia Lange Designs

Delight a friend with this **decorative recipe card holder** to hang in his or her kitchen.
Be sure to include a favorite recipe, too!

## Skill Level • Beginner

## Materials

- 1 sheet stiff 7-count plastic canvas
- Coats & Clark Red Heart Classic worsted weight yarn Art. E267 as listed in color key
- DMC #3 pearl cotton as listed in color key
- #16 tapestry needle
- 18 inches 20-gauge white wrapped florists' wire
- 12-inch wooden spoon
- 10 inches ¼-inch-wide blue picot satin ribbon
- Soup recipe
- White paper
- Hot-glue gun

## Finished Size

7½ inches W x 5¾ inches H, excluding hanger and wooden spoon

## Instructions

**1** Cut plastic canvas according to graphs.

**2** Stitch pieces following graphs, working uncoded areas on pocket with blue jewel Continental Stitches.

**3** When background stitching is completed, use very dark coffee brown pearl cotton to work lettering on sign and on pocket. Backstitch soup ladle handle on pocket with mid brown yarn.

**4** Using mid brown yarn, Overcast

sign. Using skipper blue, Overcast recipe pocket.

**5** Using photo as a guide throughout, run a bead of glue along side and bottom edges of pocket on wrong side; press onto sign in lower right-hand corner.

**6** For hanger, wrap wire around handle of wooden spoon; remove and stretch wire to fit. Thread ends through top corner holes in sign, then wrap around wire just above sign.

**7** Tie ribbon around spoon in a bow and glue spoon to sign.

**8** Cut white paper 2⅛ inches wide. Write soup recipe on paper, writing soup name at top. Fold paper to fit in pocket so recipe name shows above pocket. #

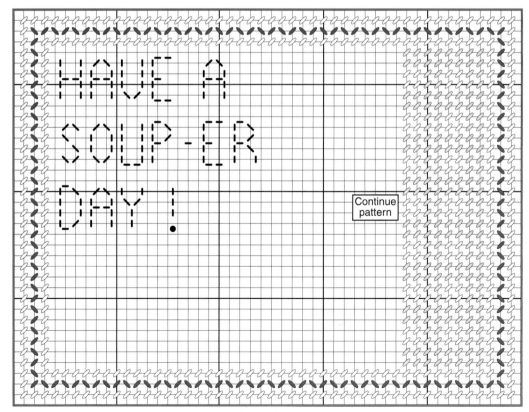

**Recipe Sign**
49 holes x 37 holes
Cut 1

## COLOR KEY

**Worsted Weight Yarn** — Yards

- ☐ White #1 — 3
- ■ Mid brown #339 — 6
- ☐ Pale blue #815 — 17
- ☐ Blue jewel #818 — 9
- ■ Skipper blue #848 — 5

  Uncoded areas on pocket are blue jewel #818 Continental Stitches
- ⁄ Mid brown #818 Backstitch

**#3 Pearl Cotton**

- ⁄ Very dark coffee brown #898 Backstitch — 3
- ● Very dark coffee brown #898 French Knot

Color numbers given are for Coats & Clark Red Heart Classic worsted weight yarn Art. E267 and DMC #3 pearl cotton.

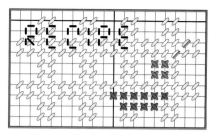

**Recipe Pocket**
19 holes x 11 holes
Cut 1

**Keepsake Egg continued from page 12**

## COLOR KEY

**#3 Pearl Cotton** — Yards

- ■ Ultra very light blue #828 — 4
- ■ Forest green #989 — 3

**6-Strand Rayon Embroidery Floss**

- ■ Violet #30553 — 3
- ☐ Medium pink #30776 — 5
- ☐ Snow white #35200 — 1
- ● Violet #30553 French Knot

**6-Strand Cotton Embroidery Floss**

- ■ Light coral #352 — 2
- ☐ Pale yellow #744 — 3

  Uncoded areas are white Continental Stitches — 6
- ⁄ White Overcasting
- ⁄ Very dark lavender #208 Backstitch — 1
- ⁄ Light coral #352 Backstitch
- ⁄ Pale yellow #744 Backstitch
- ⁄ Very light blue #827 Backstitch — 1
- ⁄ Forest green #989 Backstitch — 1
- ⁄ Very light plum #3608 Backstitch — 1
- ● Very dark lavender #208 French Knot
- ● Light coral #352 French Knot
- ○ Pale yellow #744 French Knot
- ● Very light blue #827 French Knot
- ● Forest green #989 French Knot
- ● Very light plum #3608 French Knot

**4mm Silk Ribbon**

- ⁄ Light emerald #24-642 Straight Stitch

Color numbers given are for DMC #3 pearl cotton, 6-strand rayon embroidery floss and 6-strand cotton embroidery floss, and Bucilla 4mm silk ribbon.

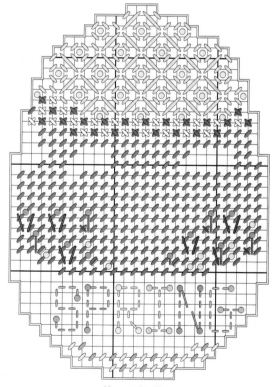

**Keepsake Egg**
25 holes x 35 holes
Cut 1

# Tasseled Bookmarks

Designs by Ronda Bryce

Whether you're sitting under a summer sky or curled up by the fireside, these distinctive bookmarks **add a vibrant touch** to your reading experience!

## Skill Level • Beginner

## Finished Size

2¼ inches W x 11 inches L, including tassels

## Materials

- 1 sheet 7-count plastic canvas
- 3 (3-inch) Uniek QuickShape plastic canvas radial circles
- Uniek Needloft plastic canvas yarn as listed in color key
- Uniek Needloft metallic craft cord as listed in color key
- Uniek Needloft iridescent craft cord as listed in color key
- DMC 6-strand embroidery floss as listed in color key
- #16 tapestry needle
- 3 (½-inch) white ribbon roses
- 23 black seed beads
- 11 (4mm) round gold beads
- Small gold star charm or bead
- 3 (3-inch) red tassels
- Hand-sewing needle
- Red, black, brown, white and green sewing thread
- Brown chenille stem
- Pliers (optional)
- Hot-glue gun

## Cutting & Stitching

**1** Cut bookmarks from plastic canvas according to graphs (pages 17 and 18).

**2** Stitch and Overcast bookmarks following graphs, working Continental Stitches in uncoded areas as follows: on watermelon, Christmas red in center and Christmas green on border; on pumpkin, bittersweet for background; on Christmas, fern on background.

**3** When Continental Stitches and Overcasting are completed, work Backstitches on pumpkin with black brown embroidery floss.

**4** For each bookmark, cut one complete quarter section from one plastic canvas circle, discarding remainder of piece.

**5** For watermelon slice, Continenta Stitch quarter section from outer row to center as follows: first row with fern, second row with white, next two rows with red and remaining four rows with Christmas red. Overcast edges of red areas with Christmas red and remaining edges with holly.

**6** For pumpkin pie slice, Continental Stitch quarter section

as follows: first outside row with brown and remaining rows with rust. Overcast edges with adjacent colors.

**7** For Christmas tree, Continental Stitch quarter section from outer row to center as follows: first two rows with Christmas green, next three rows with fern and remaining three rows with moss. Overcast edges with Christmas green.

## Finishing

**1** Using hand-sewing needle and black sewing thread, attach seed beads to red areas of watermelon slice.

**2** Using tapestry needle, attach tassel hanger to a center top hole of bookmark with a Lark's Head Knot. Using hand-sewing needle and red thread, tack slice to tassel.

**3** Bend chenille stem to make scallops; cut to fit curved edge of pie slice. Using hand-sewing needle and brown thread, stitch scalloped stem to slice.

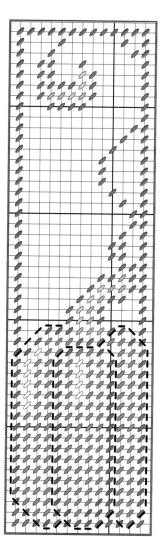

**Pumpkin Bookmark**
14 holes x 48 holes
Cut 1

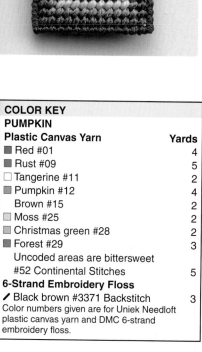

**COLOR KEY**
**PUMPKIN**

| Plastic Canvas Yarn | Yards |
|---|---|
| ■ Red #01 | 4 |
| ■ Rust #09 | 5 |
| □ Tangerine #11 | 2 |
| ■ Pumpkin #12 | 4 |
| Brown #15 | 2 |
| ■ Moss #25 | 2 |
| ■ Christmas green #28 | 2 |
| ■ Forest #29 | 3 |
| Uncoded areas are bittersweet #52 Continental Stitches | 5 |

**6-Strand Embroidery Floss**

| | |
|---|---|
| ✗ Black brown #3371 Backstitch | 3 |

Color numbers given are for Uniek Needloft plastic canvas yarn and DMC 6-strand embroidery floss.

**4** Using hand-sewing needle and white sewing thread, attach white ribbon roses to center of pumpkin quarter section.

**5** Attach tassel to bookmark as in step 2, then tack pie slice to tassel with red thread.

**6** Using hand-sewing needle and green sewing thread, attach gold beads to Christmas tree as desired, then sew or glue gold star to top of tree.

**7** Attach tassel to bookmark as in step 2, then tack tree to tassel with red thread. #

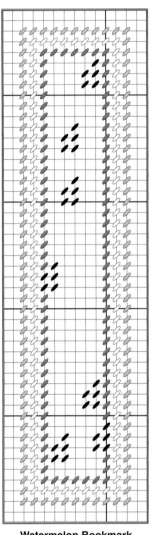

| COLOR KEY | |
|---|---|
| **WATERMELON** | |
| **Plastic Canvas Yarn** | **Yards** |
| ■ Red #01 | 4 |
| ▨ Fern #23 | 4 |
| ☐ White #41 | 4 |
| Uncoded area in center is Christmas red #02 Continental Stitches | 5 |
| Uncoded area on border is Christmas green #28 Continental Stitches | 3 |
| ⁄ Holly #27 Overcasting | 3 |
| **Metallic Craft Cord** | |
| ■ Black #55000 | 2 |
| Color numbers given are for Uniek Needloft plastic canvas yarn and metallic craft cord. | |

| COLOR KEY | |
|---|---|
| **CHRISTMAS** | |
| **Plastic Canvas Yarn** | **Yards** |
| ■ Red #01 | 4 |
| ☐ Christmas red #02 | 3 |
| ▨ Moss #25 | 4 |
| ■ Christmas green #28 | 7 |
| Uncoded areas are fern #23 Continental Stitches | 5 |
| **Iridescent Craft Cord** | |
| ☐ White #55033 | 5 |
| Color numbers given are for Uniek Needloft plastic canvas yarn and iridescent craft cord. | |

**Watermelon Bookmark**
14 holes x 48 holes
Cut 1

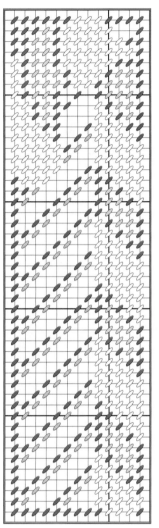

**Christmas Bookmark**
14 holes x 48 holes
Cut 1

# Frosty Family Wall Hanging

Design by Janelle Giese

This rosy-cheeked **family of snow people** will put you in a festive mood,
perfect for Christmas caroling on a snowy winter's night!

## Finished Size

10⅝ inches W x 13½ inches H

## Materials

- 1 sheet 7-count plastic canvas
- Coats & Clark Red Heart Classic worsted weight yarn Art. E267 as listed in color key
- DMC 6-strand embroidery floss: small amount white and as listed in color key
- DMC #5 pearl cotton as listed in color key
- #16 tapestry needle
- Sawtooth hanger

## Instructions

**1** Cut plastic canvas according to graph.

**2** Stitch and Overcast piece following graph with Continental Stitches and Slanted Gobelin Stitches, working uncoded areas with white Continental Stitches.

**3** When background stitching is completed, work black yarn Straight Stitches for eyes on lady and child, passing over lady's eyes three times and child's eyes two times. Straight Stitch eye highlights on all snow people with white yarn, piercing through center of embroidered pupils.

**4** Straight Stitch fringe of scarf with light sage yarn. Cross Stitch cheeks with 2 plies light melon floss. Work remaining embroidery with black pearl cotton, wrapping pearl cotton one time around needle for bird's French Knot eyes.

**5** Sew sawtooth hanger to center backside at cheek area, using 2 plies white floss. #

| COLOR KEY | |
|---|---|
| **Worsted Weight Yarn** | **Yards** |
| ✐ Black #12 | 6 |
| △ Cornmeal #220 | 1 |
| ♡ Sea coral #246 | 4 |
| ■ Medium coral #252 | 3 |
| ◇ Silver #412 | 1 |
| ✐ Light plum #531 | 4 |
| ▽ Light lavender #579 | 3 |
| ⟋ Light sage #631 | 5 |
| ✐ Dark sage #633 | 5 |
| ⟋ Lily pink #719 | 3 |
| ✐ Pale rose #755 | 2 |
| ✐ Cameo rose #759 | 2 |
| ⟋ Pale blue #815 | 17 |
| ◆ Light periwinkle #827 | 1 |
| Uncoded areas are white #1 Continental Stitches | 41 |
| ⟋ White #1 Straight Stitch and Overcasting | |
| ✐ Black #12 Straight Stitch | |
| ⟋ Light sage #631 Straight Stitch | |
| **6-Strand Embroidery Floss** | |
| ✕ Light melon #3708 Cross Stitch | 1 |
| **#5 Pearl Cotton** | |
| ⟋ Black #310 Backstitch and Straight Stitch | 17 |
| ● Black #310 French Knot | |
| Color numbers given are for Coats & Clark Red Heart Classic worsted weight yarn Art. E267 and DMC 6-strand embroidery floss and #5 pearl cotton. | |

**Frosty Family**
70 holes x 89 holes
Cut 1

# Sweet Millie Mouse Air Freshener Cover

Design by Judy Collishaw

This well-mannered mouse is **all dressed up** and ready to make any room as sweet and delightful as a breath of fresh air!

## Skill Level • Intermediate

## Finished Size

6 inches W x 8½ inches H x 4 inches D

## Materials

- 2 sheets 7-count plastic canvas
- Worsted weight yarn as listed in color key
- DMC #5 pearl cotton as listed in color key
- #16 tapestry needle
- 2 (9mm) round black cabochons
- 9 inches ¼-inch-wide white satin ribbon
- 24 inches ¾-inch-wide white gathered lace
- Low-temperature glue gun

## Cutting & Stitching

**1** Cut plastic canvas according to graphs (page 24). Cut one 2-hole x 29-hole piece for basket handle.

**2** Continental Stitch and Overcast handle with copper. Stitch and Overcast head, ears, arms and feet following graphs, working uncoded areas on head, arms and feet with gray Continental Stitches and reversing one arm before stitching.

**3** Stitch body pieces and basket sides, working uncoded areas on body pieces with white Continental Stitches. Overcast top edges of basket sides and bottom edges of body pieces.

**4** Work embroidery on head, arms and body pieces when background stitching and Overcasting are completed.

**5** Whipstitch body pieces together along side edges, easing at top to fit; Overcast top edges. Whipstitch wrong sides of basket sides together around side and bottom edges.

## Assembly

**1** Glue lace around sides and top of head from arrow to arrow, easing around top of head; trim excess. Glue ears to head behind lace at top corners (see photo). Glue second length of lace to back of head behind ears from arrow to arrow; trim excess as needed.

**2** Glue head to top of body with chin about 1 inch from top. For eyes, glue cabochons to face above nose. Tie white satin ribbon in a bow and glue under chin; trim as desired.

**3** Glue edge of each foot to bottom edge of body front sides. *Note: Make sure to glue only the edges together to allow room for air freshener to be inserted.*

**4** Using white yarn, tack top of sleeves to side edges of body, matching blue dots.

**5** Glue handle ends inside basket. Slip handle over arm, then glue wrist to front edge of body, holding basket in place. #

| COLOR KEY | |
|---|---|
| **Worsted Weight Yarn** | **Yards** |
| ☐ White | 30 |
| ☐ Gray | 17 |
| ☐ Rose | 7 |
| ☐ Dark rose | 4 |
| ☐ Copper | 1 |
| ☐ Black | 1 |
| ☐ Brown | 1 |
| Uncoded areas on body pieces are white Continental Stitches | |
| Uncoded areas on head, arms and feet are gray Continental Stitches | |
| **#5 Pearl Cotton** | |
| ✐ Black #310 Backstitch and Straight Stitch | 1 |
| ✐ Very dark emerald green #909 Straight Stitch | 5 |
| Color numbers given are for DMC #5 pearl cotton. | |

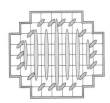

**Mouse Ear**
9 holes x 8 holes
Cut 2

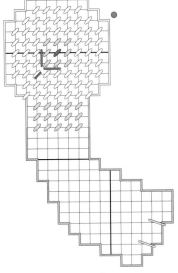

**Mouse Arm**
16 holes x 25 holes
Cut 2, reverse 1

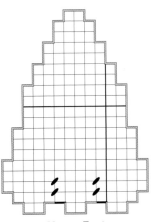

**Mouse Foot**
14 holes x 19 holes
Cut 2

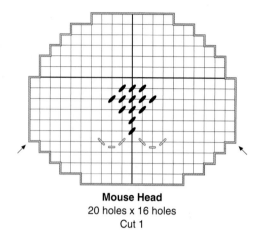

**Mouse Head**
20 holes x 16 holes
Cut 1

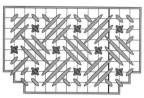

**Basket Side**
13 holes x 8 holes
Cut 2

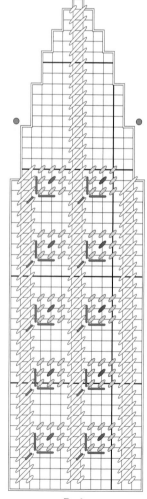

**Body**
13 holes x 46 holes
Cut 5

| COLOR KEY | |
|---|---|
| **Worsted Weight Yarn** | **Yards** |
| ☐ White | 30 |
| ▨ Gray | 17 |
| ☐ Rose | 7 |
| ▨ Dark rose | 4 |
| ▨ Copper | 1 |
| ■ Black | 1 |
| ▨ Brown | 1 |
| Uncoded areas on body pieces are white Continental Stitches | |
| Uncoded areas on head, arms and feet are gray Continental Stitches | |
| **#5 Pearl Cotton** | |
| ╱ Black #310 Backstitch and Straight Stitch | 1 |
| ╱ Very dark emerald green #909 Straight Stitch | 5 |
| Color numbers given are for DMC #5 pearl cotton. | |

# Birthday Pin

Design by Cynthia Roberts

Give your **guest of honor** a proud feeling of specialness with this celebratory pin!

## Skill Level • Beginner

## Finished Size

2½ inches W x 2⅜ inches H

## Materials

- ¼ sheet 10-count plastic canvas
- 6-strand embroidery floss as listed in color key
- #22 tapestry needle
- 4-inch square white adhesive-backed felt
- 1-inch pin back
- Hot-glue gun

## Instructions

**1** Cut plastic canvas according to graph.

**2** Stitch and Overcast piece following graph, working uncoded area with white Continental Stitches.

**3** When background stitching is completed, work lettering with 2 plies blue floss.

**4** Using 6 plies black floss through step 6, for each balloon tie, work Straight Stitch from right to left at bottom of balloon where indicated, then bring floss back up through hole on right and leave a 3-inch tail.

**5** Bring ends of a 6-inch length floss from back to front through holes indicated with black dots and tie around balloon tails; trim ends.

**6** Cut felt to fit pin; adhere to backside. Glue pin back to top backside of pin. #

**Birthday Pin**
25 holes x 23 holes
Cut 1

| COLOR KEY | |
|---|---|
| **6-Strand Embroidery Floss** | **Yards** |
| ■ Red | 3 |
| ■ Blue | 2 |
| □ Yellow | 1 |
| Uncoded area is white Continental Stitches | 6 |
| ╱ Blue (2-ply) Backstitch and Straight Stitch | |
| ╱ Black Straight Stitch | 1 |

# Sunshine Quilt Block Organizer

Design by Debra Arch

The cheerful **charm of this decorative organizer** will help you
store important items in cool country style!

## Skill Level • Beginner

## Finished Size

10 inches W x 10 inches H

## Materials

- 2 sheets stiff 7-count plastic canvas
- Coats & Clark Red Heart Classic worsted weight yarn Art. E267 as listed in color key
- #16 tapestry needle
- 20-inch square light-weight iron-on facing
- 3-inch x 6-inch piece white felt
- 8 (¾-inch) round magnets
- Hot-glue gun

## Instructions

**1** Cut plastic canvas according to graph. Back piece will remain unstitched.

**2** Stitch front piece following graph, working vertical and horizontal stitches with two strands yarn. Remaining stitching should be worked with one strand yarn.

**3** Overcast top edge with true blue. Place iron-on facing, adhesive side down, on backside of stitched piece; iron with warm iron to fuse in place.

**4** Using true blue, Whipstitch front and back together around side and bottom edges.

**5** Cut eight 1¼-inch squares from white felt, then glue evenly spaced across top and bottom of unstitched back. Glue one magnet to each felt square. #

| COLOR KEY | |
|---|---|
| **Worsted Weight Yarn** | **Yards** |
| ☐ White #1 | 30 |
| ▨ Cornmeal #220 | 20 |
| ☐ Maize #261 | 10 |
| ☐ Blue jewel #818 | 20 |
| ■ True blue #822 | 20 |
| Color numbers given are for Coats & Clark Red Heart Classic worsted weight yarn Art. E267. | |

**Quilt Block Front & Back**
66 holes x 66 holes
Cut 2

# Blue Willow Tissue Box

Design by Joan Green

Like painted porcelain or your finest china, this delicately detailed tissue topper adds antique elegance to any room!

## Skill Level • Beginner

## Finished Size

Fits boutique-style tissue box

## Materials

- 1¼ sheets 7-count plastic canvas
- Worsted weight yarn as listed in color key
- #16 tapestry needle

## Instructions

**1** Cut plastic canvas according to graphs.

**2** Stitch pieces following graphs, working uncoded areas with winter white Continental Stitches.

**3** When background stitching is completed, Backstitch stems and leaves of flowers with full strand of medium navy.

**4** Backstitch scroll designs on sides and around opening on top with 2 plies light navy. Work all remaining embroidery with 2 plies medium navy.

**5** Using full strand of medium navy throughout, Overcast opening on top. Whipstitch sides together, then Whipstitch sides to top; Overcast bottom edges. #

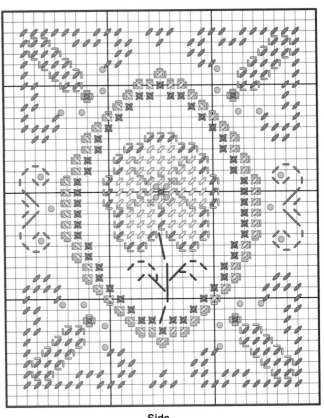

**Side**
30 holes x 37 holes
Cut 4

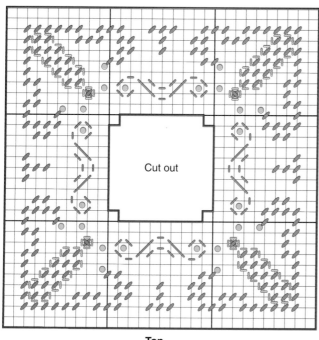

**Top**
30 holes x 30 holes
Cut 1

| COLOR KEY | |
|---|---|
| **Worsted Weight Yarn** | **Yards** |
| ■ Light navy | 28 |
| □ Pale navy | 10 |
| Uncoded areas are winter white Continental Stitches | 50 |
| ✏ Medium navy 4-ply Backstitch, Overcasting and Whipstitching | 20 |
| ✏ Medium navy 2-ply Backstitch | |
| ✏ Light navy 2-ply Backstitch | |
| ● Medium navy 2-ply French Knot | |

## Finished Size

5 inches W x 7 inches H

## Materials

- ½ sheet 10-count plastic canvas
- DMC #3 pearl cotton as listed in color key
- Metallic ribbon floss from Rhode Island Textile Co. as listed in color key
- #18 tapestry needle
- 1-inch round mirror
- 6 inches ⅛-inch-wide dark green ribbon
- 5-inch x 7-inch piece thin cardboard (optional)
- 5-inch x 7-inch picture frame
- Hot-glue gun

## Instructions

**1** Cut plastic canvas according to graph.

**2** Stitch piece following graph, working only inside the blue highlighted bars and working uncoded background with white Continental Stitches.

**3** Glue 1-inch round mirror to piece where indicated on graph. Tie ribbon in a small bow; glue or stitch above mirror (see photo).

**4** Place stitched piece in frame without glass, backing with cardboard if needed. #

# Daughter's Lament

Design by Alida Macor

This **witty wall hanging**, with its lighthearted charm, will help you look on the bright side of life!

| COLOR KEY | |
|---|---|
| **#3 Pearl Cotton** | **Yards** |
| ▨ Medium pink #776 | 3 |
| ▢ Medium nile green #913 | 2 |
| ▧ Hunter green #3346 | 4 |
| ▢ Light yellow green #3348 | 5 |
| Uncoded background is white Continental Stitches | 35 |
| **Metallic Ribbon Floss** | |
| ▨ Gold #144F-1 | 2 |
| ● Attach mirror | |
| Color numbers given are for DMC #3 pearl cotton and Rhode Island Textile Co. RibbonFloss. | |

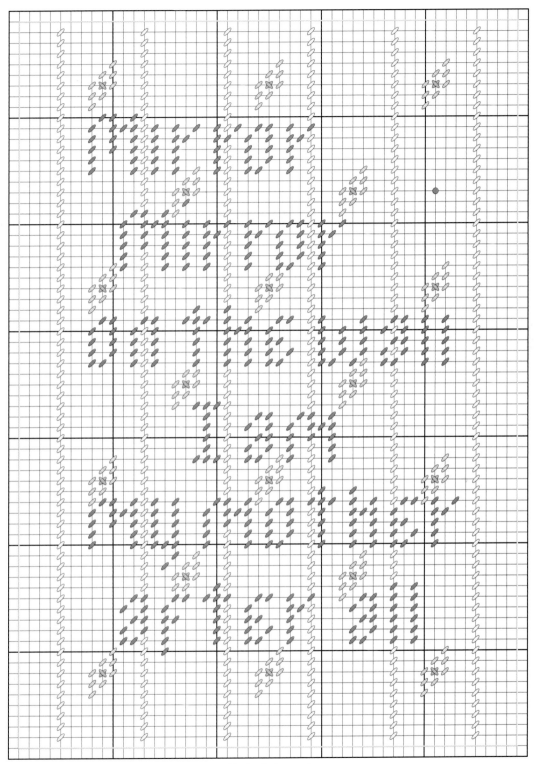

**Mother's Lament**
50 holes x 70 holes
Cut 1

# CHAPTER TWO

# Gobelin Stitch

## Fun and easy, the Gobelin Stitch makes any project enjoyable!

**Straight Gobelin Stitch**

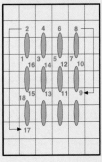

**Slanted Gobelin Stitch**

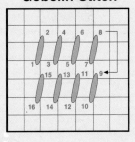

**Slanted Gobelin**

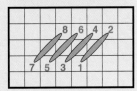

Here you'll find practical projects for home accents of all types, from decorative to functional, from casual to formal, each featuring this popular stitch!

# Amish Quilt Tissue Box Cover

Design by Kathy Wirth

Like a treasured heirloom quilt, this quaintly styled tissue topper will bring lovely old-world charm to any room!

### Skill level • Beginner

**Finished Size**

Fits boutique-style tissue box

## Materials

- 1½ sheets stiff 7-count plastic canvas
- Coats & Clark Red Heart Classic worsted weight yarn Art. E267 as listed in color key
- #16 tapestry needle

## Instructions

**1** Cut plastic canvas according to graphs.

**2** Stitch pieces following graphs, working uncoded areas with black Continental Stitches.

**3** When background stitching is completed, work country red French Knot in center of each side motif.

**4** Using black throughout, Overcast inside edges of top and bottom edges of sides. Whipstitch sides together, then Whipstitch sides to top. #

| COLOR KEY | |
|---|---|
| **Worsted Weight Yarn** | **Yards** |
| ☐ Medium coral #252 | 20 |
| ■ Peacock green #508 | 20 |
| ☐ Mist green #681 | 20 |
| ■ Country red #914 | 20 |
| Uncoded areas are black #12 Continental Stitches | 13 |
| ╱ Black #12 Overcasting and Whipstitching | |
| ● Country red #914 French Knot | |

Color numbers given are for Coats & Clark Red Heart Classic worsted weight yarn Art. E267.

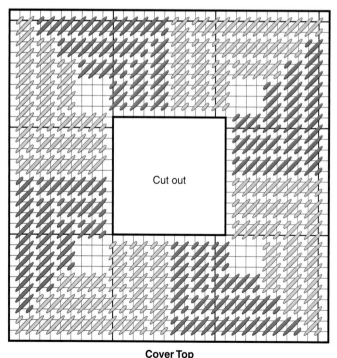

**Cover Top**
31 holes x 31 holes
Cut 1

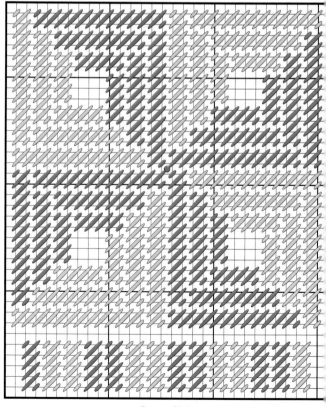

**Cover Side**
31 holes x 37 holes
Cut 4

# Sparkle Butterflies

Designs by Kristine Loffredo

These beautiful butterflies, with their glittering wings, appear to be fluttering on a summer breeze!

## Skill level • Beginner

## Finished Size

**Small Butterfly:** 3¾ W inches x 3½ inches H

**Medium Butterfly:** 3¾ W inches x 4¼ inches H

**Large Butterfly:** 5 inches W x 4⅝ inches H

## Materials

- 1 sheet Uniek QuickCount pastel green 7-count plastic canvas
- Uniek Needloft iridescent craft cord as listed in color key
- #16 tapestry needle
- 4 inches ½-inch-wide magnet strip
- Hot-glue gun

## Instructions

**1** Cut and stitch plastic canvas according to graphs (page 53).

**2** Whipstitch right sides of corresponding butterfly wings together along inside edges from blue dot to blue dot; Overcast all remaining edges.

**3** Cut magnet strip in one 1-inch and two 1½-inch pieces. Center and glue 1-inch strip to back of small butterfly along joining seam. Repeat with remaining two magnet strips, gluing to backs of medium and large butterflies. #

# Watermelon Pinwheel Table Set

*Designs by Angie Arickx*

Put your family in the mood for a sweet summer snack with this cheerful collection of watermelon accents!

## Skill level • Beginner

## Finished Size

**Place Mat:** 16 inches W x 10¾ inches H

**Napkin Holder:** 6⅝ inches W x 3⅞ inches H x 2⅛ inches D

**Coasters:** 3⅞ inches square

**Coaster Holder:** 4¼ inches W x 2 inches H x 1½ inches D

## Materials

- 1 sheet artist-size soft 7-count plastic canvas
- 2 sheets regular-size stiff 7-count plastic canvas
- Uniek Needloft plastic canvas yarn as listed in color key
- #16 tapestry needle
- Hot-glue gun

## Project Note

For each additional place mat you will need approximately 5 yards of black, 28 of fern, 13 of holly, 51 of white and 19 of watermelon.

## Instructions

**1** Cut place mat from soft plastic canvas; cut remaining pieces from stiff plastic canvas according to graphs (this page and pages 38 and 39).

**2** Cut one 43-hole x 13-hole piece for napkin holder bottom and one 27-hole x 9-hole piece for coaster holder bottom from stiff plastic canvas. Bottom pieces will remain unstitched.

**3** Stitch pieces following graphs, working left side of place mat to midpoint. Turn graph 180 degrees and continue stitching.

**4** Using white through step 5, Overcast place mat, coasters and top edges of all holder front, back and side pieces.

**5** For each holder, Whipstitch front and back to sides, then Whipstitch front, back and sides to unstitched bottom. #

| COLOR KEY | |
|---|---|
| **Plastic Canvas Yarn** | **Yards** |
| ■ Black #00 | 9 |
| ■ Fern #23 | 67 |
| ■ Holly #27 | 24 |
| □ White #41 | 100 |
| ■ Watermelon #55 | 37 |
| Color numbers given are for Uniek Needloft plastic canvas yarn. | |

**Coaster Holder Side**
9 holes x 13 holes
Cut 2 from stiff

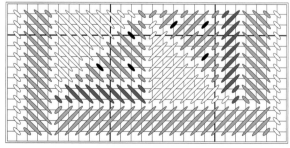

**Coaster Holder Front & Back**
27 holes x 13 holes
Cut 2 from stiff

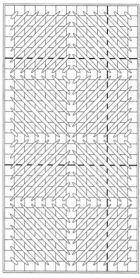

**Napkin Holder Side**
13 holes x 25 holes
Cut 2 from stiff

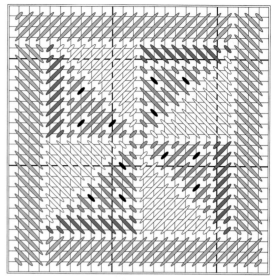

**Coaster**
25 holes x 25 holes
Cut 4 from stiff

| COLOR KEY | |
|---|---|
| **Plastic Canvas Yarn** | **Yards** |
| ■ Black #00 | 9 |
| ▨ Fern #23 | 67 |
| ■ Holly #27 | 24 |
| □ White #41 | 100 |
| ▨ Watermelon #55 | 37 |
| Color numbers given are for Uniek Needloft plastic canvas yarn. | |

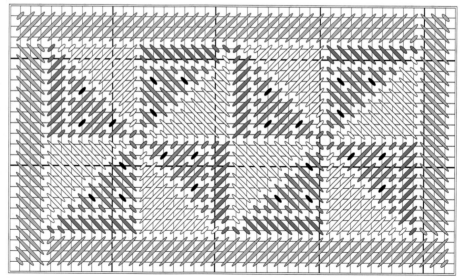

**Napkin Holder Front & Back**
43 holes x 25 holes
Cut 2 from stiff

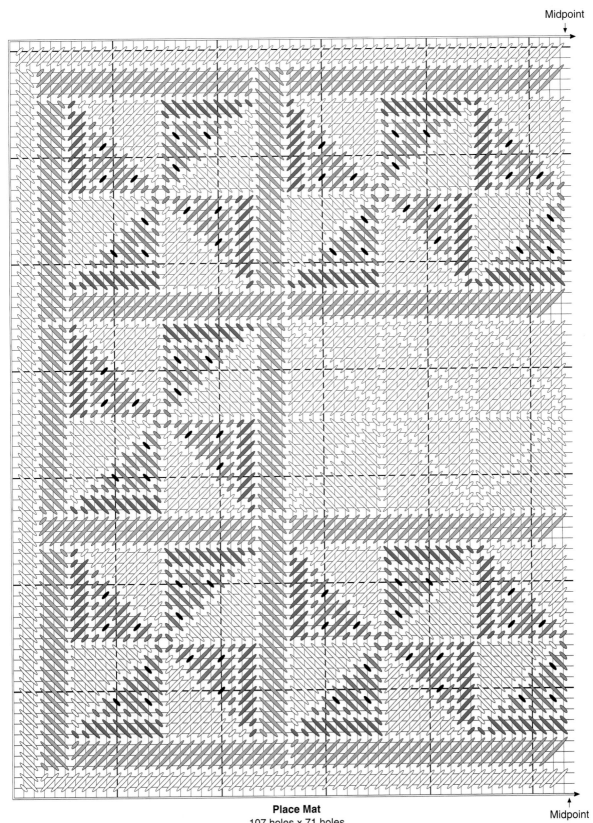

**Place Mat**
107 holes x 71 holes
Cut 1 from soft
Stitch left half as graphed
Turn graph 180 degrees
and stitch right half

# Little Miss Ladybug & Frog Prince

*Designs by Kristine Loffredo*

Give your home a **lively garden flair** with the freshness of these whimsical creature planters!

## Skill level • Intermediate

## Finished Size

**Ladybug:** 6¾ inches W x 5¾ inches L x 6 inches H, including antennae

**Frog:** 9 inches W x 6½ inches L x 4⅛ inches H

## Materials

**Each planter**

- 1 sheet stiff 7-count plastic canvas
- 2 (6-inch) plastic canvas radial circles
- Uniek Needloft plastic canvas yarn as listed in color key
- #16 tapestry needle
- Hot-glue gun

**Ladybug**

- Black chenille stem
- Pencil

## Instructions

**1** Cut body fronts and backs from plastic canvas radial circles (page 44), cutting away gray areas. Cut one 38-hole x 30-hole piece from stiff plastic canvas for each body base. Bases will remain unstitched.

**2** Cut remaining pieces from stiff plastic canvas according to graphs (pages 42 and 43).

**3** Stitch and Overcast heads following graphs, working uncoded area on ladybug head with white Continental Stitches and uncoded area on frog head with Christmas green Continental Stitches. Work embroidery when background stitching and Overcasting are completed.

**4** Stitch remaining pieces following graphs, reversing two frog feet before stitching and working uncoded areas on frog pieces with Christmas green Continental Stitches.

**5** Using black, Overcast ladybug front legs and all but long straight side edge of each side leg. Overcast inside edges of ladybug body with red. Overcast frog feet and inside edges of body with Christmas green.

**6** For each planter, Whipstitch bottom edges of body front and back to long edges of unstitched body base. Whipstitch body to curved edges of front and back, easing as necessary to fit, then Whipstitch side edges of body to remaining edges of base.

**7** For ladybug antennae, cut black chenille stem in half. Wrap each half around pencil to coil. Remove pencil and twist one end of each antenna so end is hidden. Thread other ends from front to back through holes indicated with blue dots. Bend ends up and glue to secure.

**8** Using photo as a guide through step 9, center and glue unstitched edges of side feet to base on each side of ladybug. Glue front feet to base with 1 inch extending in front. Glue head at a slight angle to body front.

**9** For frog, glue two feet to bottom of base with 2 inches extending in front. Glue remaining two feet to base on each side of body near back, allowing 1¾ inches to extend from sides. Center and glue head to front. #

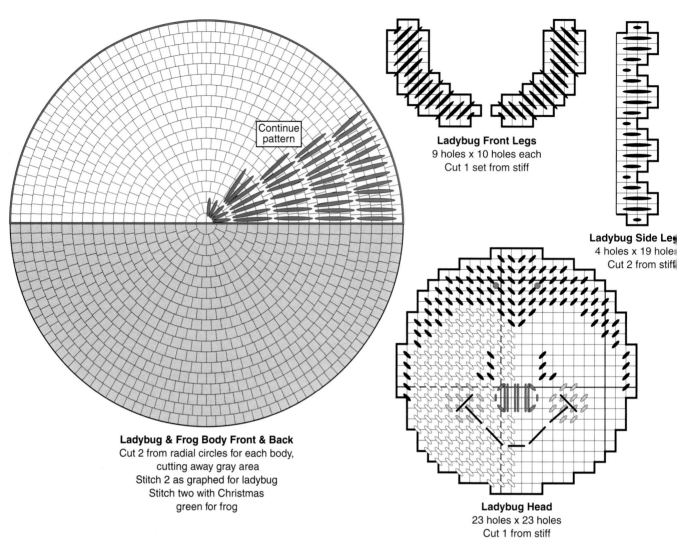

Continue pattern

**Ladybug Front Legs**
9 holes x 10 holes each
Cut 1 set from stiff

**Ladybug Side Leg**
4 holes x 19 holes
Cut 2 from stiff

**Ladybug & Frog Body Front & Back**
Cut 2 from radial circles for each body,
cutting away gray area
Stitch 2 as graphed for ladybug
Stitch two with Christmas
green for frog

**Ladybug Head**
23 holes x 23 holes
Cut 1 from stiff

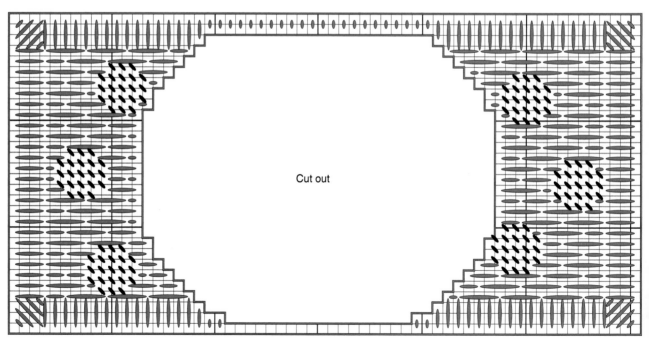

Cut out

**Ladybug Body**
61 holes x 30 holes
Cut 1 from stiff

## COLOR KEY

| Plastic Canvas Yarn | Yards |
|---|---|
| ■ Black #00 | 14 |
| ■ Red #01 | 23 |
| □ Fern #23 | 5 |
| ■ Christmas green #28 | 55 |
| □ Orchid #44 | 1 |
| Uncoded areas on frog pieces are Christmas green #28 Continental Stitches | |
| Uncoded area on ladybug face is is white #41 Continental Stitches | 5 |
| ⁄ Black #00 Backstitch and Straight Stitch | |
| ⁄ Red #01 Backstitch | |
| ⁄ Pumpkin #12 Backstitch and Straight Stitch | 1 |

Color numbers given are for Uniek Needloft plastic canvas yarn.

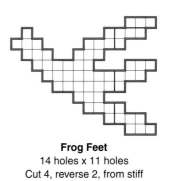

**Frog Feet**
14 holes x 11 holes
Cut 4, reverse 2, from stiff

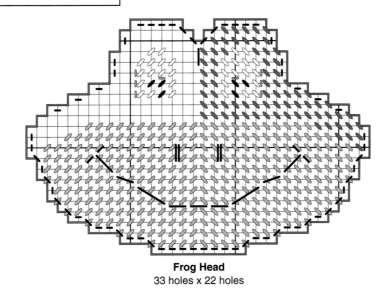

**Frog Head**
33 holes x 22 holes
Cut 1 from stiff

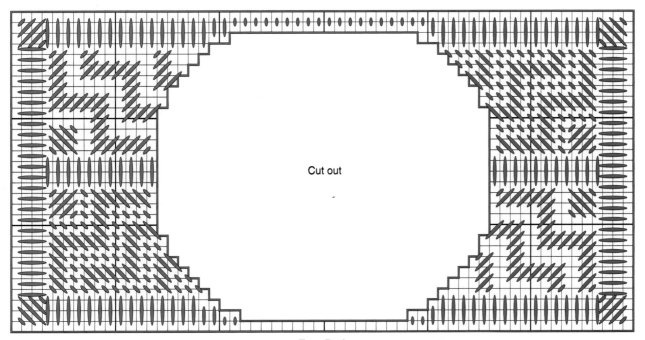

Cut out

**Frog Body**
60 holes x 30 holes
Cut 1 from stiff

# Americana Picnic Basket Tissue Topper

Design by Angie Arickx

This handsomely colored tissue topper makes the perfect
patriotic statement in your den or family room!

## Finished Size

Fits regular-size tissue box

## Materials

- 1½ sheets 7-count plastic canvas
- Uniek Needloft plastic canvas yarn as listed in color key
- Uniek Needloft metallic craft cord as listed in color key
- #16 tapestry needle
- Hot-glue gun

## Instructions

**1** Cut plastic canvas according to graphs (this page and page 46).

**2** Stitch pieces following graphs. Overcast bottom edges of sides and inside edges of top.

**3** For each handle, Whipstitch short edges of section A to both sides of section B; Overcast remaining edges of handles. Add solid gold French Knots to section A pieces where indicated on graph.

**4** Whipstitch long sides to short sides, then Whipstitch sides to top.

**5** Using photo as a guide, glue handles to sides. #

| COLOR KEY | |
|---|---|
| **Plastic Canvas Yarn** | **Yards** |
| ■ Burgundy #03 | 21 |
| □ Eggshell #39 | 23 |
| ▨ Camel #43 | 62 |
| ■ Dark royal #48 | 20 |
| **Metallic Craft Cord** | |
| ○ Solid gold #55020 French Knot | 1 |
| Color numbers given are for Uniek Needloft plastic canvas yarn and metallic craft cord. | |

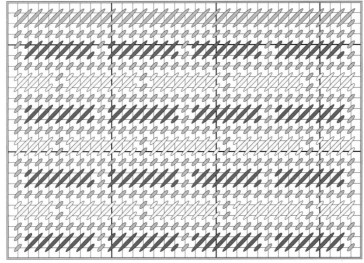

**Basket Short Side**
34 holes x 24 holes
Cut 2

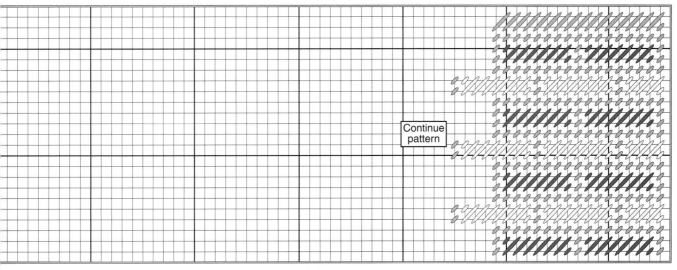

Continue
pattern

**Basket Long Side**
66 holes x 24 holes
Cut 2

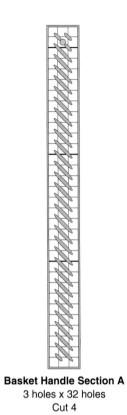

**Basket Handle Section A**
3 holes x 32 holes
Cut 4

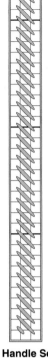

**Basket Handle Section B**
3 holes x 35 holes
Cut 2

**COLOR KEY**

| Plastic Canvas Yarn | Yards |
|---|---|
| ■ Burgundy #03 | 21 |
| □ Eggshell #39 | 23 |
| ▨ Camel #43 | 62 |
| ■ Dark royal #48 | 20 |
| **Metallic Craft Cord** | |
| ◎ Solid gold #55020 French Knot | 1 |

Color numbers given are for Uniek Needloft plastic canvas yarn and metallic craft cord.

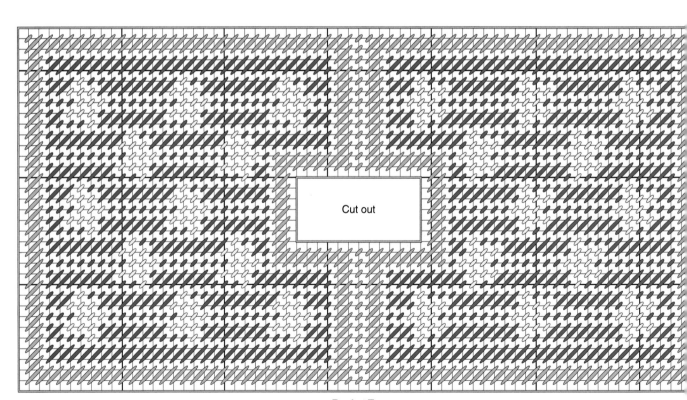

Cut out

**Basket Top**
66 holes x 34 holes
Cut 1

# Stars & Stripes Wallet Key Chain

Design by Ronda Bryce

Enjoy the festive glory of this multipurpose piece and let freedom ring wherever you go!

## Skill level • Beginner

### Finished Size

4¾ inches W x 3½ inches H

## Materials

- ½ sheet 7-count plastic canvas
- Uniek Needloft plastic canvas yarn as listed in color key
- #16 tapestry needle
- 1-inch red heart button
- ⅝-inch star buttons: 1 red and 2 white
- 25mm gold split key ring
- 4 inches ⅝-inch-wide hook-and-loop tape
- Hand-sewing needle
- Red, white and navy sewing thread

## Instructions

**1** Cut and stitch plastic canvas according to graphs (page 51).

**2** Using hand-sewing needle and white thread, sew hook side of hook-and-loop tape to top of front below top edge.

**3** Using red yarn throughout, Overcast top edge of front. Whipstitch wrong sides of front and back together, around side and bottom edges; Overcast side edges between arrows on back while Whipstitching.

**4** Using dark royal throughout, Whipstitch top edge of back to flap top, then Whipstitch flap top to flap front. Overcast remaining edges.

**5** Using hand-sewing needle and navy thread, sew loop side of hook-and-loop tape to wrong side of flap front, covering the second and third rows of stitches from the top.

**6** Using matching thread, sew three star buttons to upper left corner of flap front; sew red heart button to center front of flap front (see photo).

**7** Insert key ring through a top left hole on wallet back. #

| COLOR KEY | |
|---|---|
| **Plastic Canvas Yarn** | **Yards** |
| ■ Red #01 | 11 |
| □ White #41 | 8 |
| ■ Dark royal #48 | 6 |
| Color numbers given are for Uniek Needloft plastic canvas yarn. | |

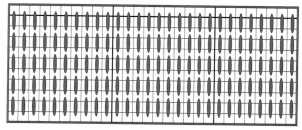

**Wallet Flap Front**
28 holes x 11 holes
Cut 1

# Pretty Posies Bathroom Set

Designs by Angie Arickx

As pretty as it is practical, this delicate set will shower your home with the soft beauty of flowers!

## Skill level • Intermediate

## Finished Size

**Vanity Tray:** 6¾ inches W x 18¾ inches L x ½ inch H

**Caddy:** 4¼ inches W x 12 inches H x 1½ inches D

**Boxes:** 3¼ inches W x 2 inches H x 3¼ inches D

## Materials

- 1¼ sheets artist-size 7-count plastic canvas
- Uniek Needloft plastic canvas yarn as listed in color key
- #16 tapestry needle
- Hot-glue gun

## Instructions

**1** Cut plastic canvas according to graphs (this page and pages 50 and 51).

**2** Following graph, stitch left side of vanity tray to midpoint, working uncoded areas with eggshell Continental Stitches. Turn graph 180 degrees and continue stitching, making sure not to repeat center row of Slanted Gobelin Stitches.

**3** Stitch remaining pieces following graphs working uncoded areas with eggshell Continental Stitches, but leaving bottom part of caddy unworked as indicated.

**4** Overcast lid top with moss. Using eggshell, Overcast lid bottom, top edges of tray sides, top edges of box sides, top and bottom edges of brush loop, top edge of caddy pocket, inside edges of caddy, and side, and top edges of caddy from blue dot to blue dot.

**5** Using eggshell through step 7, Whipstitch tray sides to tray bottom, then Whipstitch tray long sides to tray short sides.

**6** Stitch side edges of brush loop to caddy pocket where indicated with red lines. Whipstitch caddy pocket to caddy along remaining side and bottom edges.

**7** For each box, Whipstitch four box sides together, then Whipstitch sides to one box bottom.

**8** With wrong sides together, center and glue lid bottoms to lid tops. #

| COLOR KEY | |
|---|---|
| **Plastic Canvas Yarn** | **Yards** |
| ▨ Lavender #05 | 14 |
| ▧ Moss #25 | 37 |
| ▪ Forest #29 | 7 |
| ☐ Eggshell #39 | 160 |
| ☐ Yellow #57 | 3 |
| Uncoded areas are eggshell #39 Continental Stitches | |
| Color numbers given are for Uniek Needloft plastic canvas yarn. | |

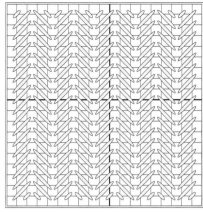

**Box Lid Bottom**
19 holes x 19 holes
Cut 2

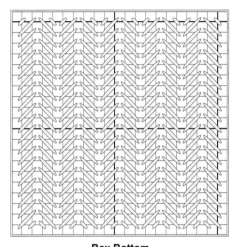

**Box Bottom**
21 holes x 21 holes
Cut 2

**Box Side**
21 holes x 11 holes
Cut 8

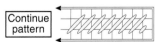

Continue pattern

**Vanity Tray Long Side**
123 holes x 3 holes
Cut 2

**Vanity Tray Short Side**
44 holes x 3 holes
Cut 2

**Caddy Brush Loop**
19 holes x 3 holes
Cut 1

Midpo →

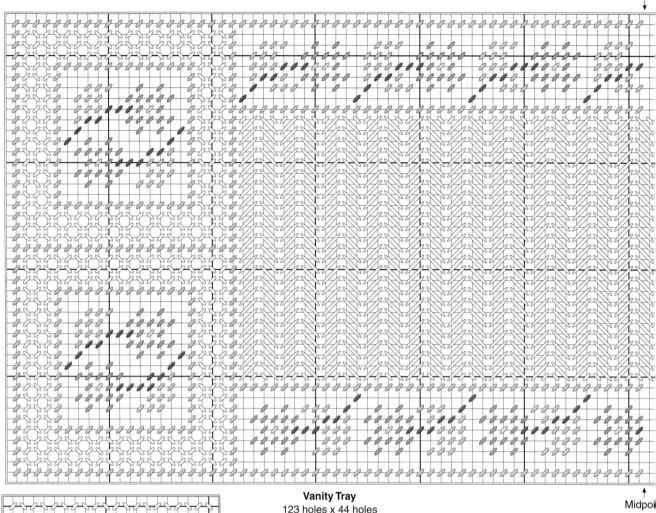

**Vanity Tray**
123 holes x 44 holes
Cut 1
Stitch left side of tray as graphed
Turn graph 180 degrees and
stitch right side of tray

↑
Midpo ►

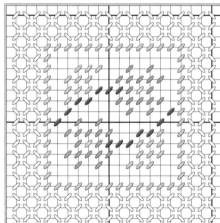

**Box Lid Top**
21 holes x 21 holes
Cut 2

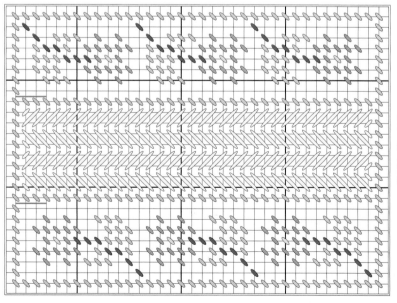

**Caddy Pocket**
27 holes x 37 holes
Cut 1

**COLOR KEY**

| Plastic Canvas Yarn | Yards |
|---|---|
| ■ Lavender #05 | 14 |
| □ Moss #25 | 37 |
| ■ Forest #29 | 7 |
| □ Eggshell #39 | 160 |
| □ Yellow #57 | 3 |

Uncoded areas are eggshell
#39 Continental Stitches
Color numbers given are for Uniek Needloft
plastic canvas yarn.

**Wallet Flap Top**
28 holes x 3 holes
Cut 1

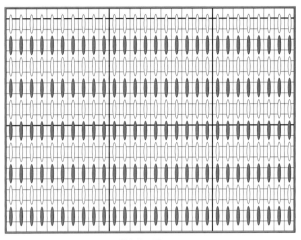

**Wallet Front**
28 holes x 21 holes
Cut 1

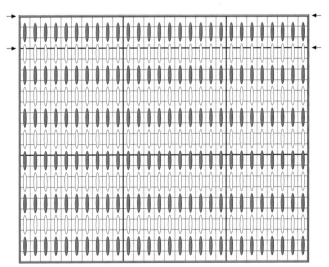

**Wallet Back**
28 holes x 23 holes
Cut 1

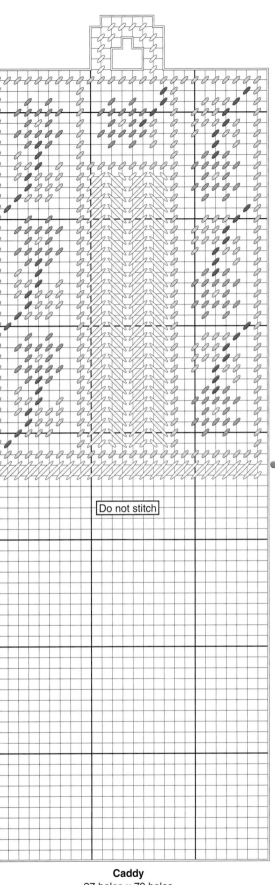

Do not stitch

**Caddy**
27 holes x 79 holes
Cut 1

| COLOR KEY | |
|---|---|
| **Plastic Canvas Yarn** | **Yards** |
| ■ Red #01 | 11 |
| □ White #41 | 8 |
| ■ Dark royal #48 | 6 |
| Color numbers given are for Uniek Needloft plastic canvas yarn. | |

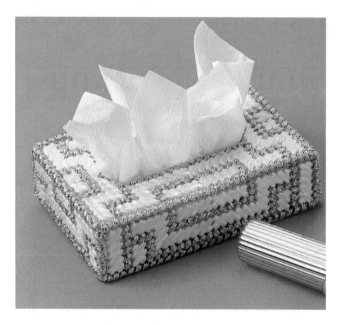

# Labyrinth Tissue Holder

Design by Kristine Loffredo

Stitch this gold-spangled tissue holder for an easy and fun addition to a night on the town!

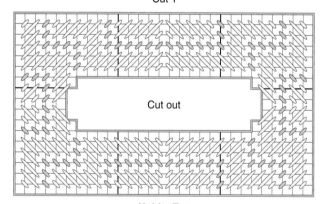

**Holder Bottom**
29 holes x 17 holes
Cut 1

**Holder Top**
29 holes x 17 holes
Cut 1

## Skill level • Beginner

### Finished Size

Fits purse-size tissue package

## Materials

- ½ sheet stiff 7-count plastic canvas
- Uniek Needloft metallic craft cord as listed in color key
- ⅛-inch-wide polyester ribbon as listed in color key
- #16 tapestry needle
- ¾-inch circle hook-and-loop tape
- Hot-glue gun

### Instructions

**1** Cut plastic canvas according to graphs. Cut one 15-hole x 5-hole piece for inside flap. Inside flap will remain unstitched.

**2** Stitch pieces following graphs. Using white/gold metallic craft cord through step 4, Overcast inside edges of top.

**3** Whipstitch top and bottom to sides, then Whipstitch one end to top, bottom and sides.

**4** Whipstitch remaining end, which will be the outside flap, to top piece only; Overcast around ide and bottom edges of this end. Center and Whipstitch inside flap to unstitched edge of bottom, Overcasting remaining edges of bottom while Whipstitching.

**5** Center and glue hook-and-loop tape to wrong side of outside flap and to the outside of the inside flap, so when flaps are closed, the tape will stick together. #

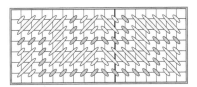

**Holder End**
17 holes x 7 holes
Cut 2

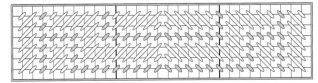

**Holder Side**
29 holes x 7 holes
Cut 2

Sparkle Butterflies continued from page 35

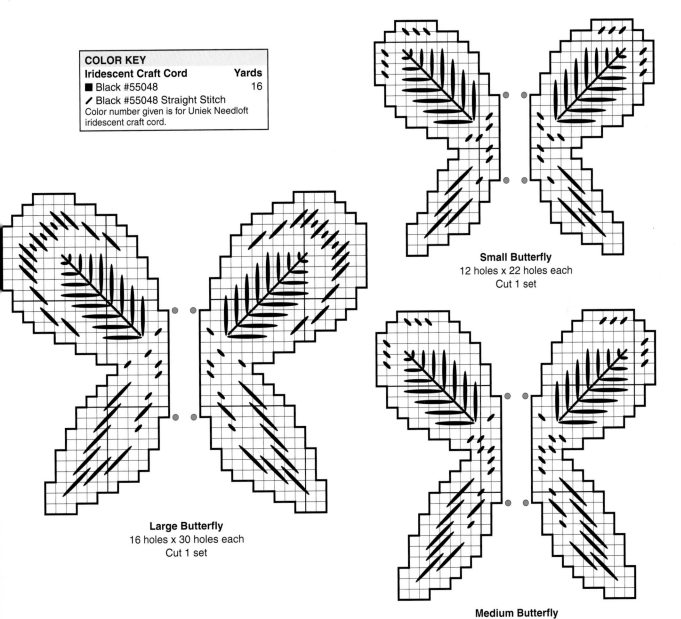

**COLOR KEY**

| Iridescent Craft Cord | Yards |
|---|---|
| ■ Black #55048 | 16 |
| ╱ Black #55048 Straight Stitch | |

Color number given is for Uniek Needloft iridescent craft cord.

**Small Butterfly**
12 holes x 22 holes each
Cut 1 set

**Large Butterfly**
16 holes x 30 holes each
Cut 1 set

**Medium Butterfly**
12 holes x 27 holes each
Cut 1 set

# CHAPTER THREE

# Straight Stitch

Straight Stitches add texture and interest to the surface of your stitching.

The popular appeal of plastic canvas is due in large part to the many different stitches that make it a fun

**Straight Stitch**

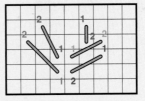

and versatile craft. In this chapter we offer you a wide selection of exciting projects that showcase the beauty, ease and simple rewards of Straight Stitches.

# Red Barn Birdhouse

Design by Patricia Everson

As charming as it is practical, this cheerful birdhouse will remind you of those good old days on the farm!

## Skill level • Advanced

## Finished Size

8 inches W x 6¼ inches H x 4⅜ inches D, excluding perch

## Materials

- 1 sheet 7-count plastic canvas
- 2 (6-inch) Uniek QuickShape plastic canvas hearts
- 3-inch plastic canvas radial circle
- Worsted weight yarn as listed in color key
- #16 tapestry needle
- 3 inches (¼-inch-diameter) dowel
- Black acrylic paint or black permanent marker
- Paintbrush
- Sandpaper or emery board
- Hot-glue gun

## Project Note

Yardage amounts may vary slightly based on individual free-form stitching.

## Windows & Perch

**1** Cut windows from plastic canvas according to graphs, cutting away gray area on round window.

**2** Stitch and Overcast windows following graphs.

**3** Carefully cut hanging tabs from hearts, keeping the circle of one.

Sand circle, then paint black with permanent marker or acrylic paint. Set aside. Painted circle will be glued around dowel later.

**4** Paint dowel black with acrylic paint or permanent marker; let dry.

## Birdhouse Stitching

**1** Cut diamond shape from front only according to graph; back will remain intact.

**2** Using photos as guides, Straight Stitch front and back with free-form stitches, beginning with various lengths of black at top to represent aging. Extend some black stitches all the way to the bottom to depict weathering boards. Work stitches down side edges to where hearts begin to curve.

**3** Continue free-form stitching with random lengths of maroon Straight Stitches under black stitches, working a few down to halfway point.

**4** Complete stitching by working various lengths of red yarn Straight Stitches, covering canvas completely.

**5** Work yellow French Knots as desired for flowers at bottom of both front and back. Work green Straight Stitches for stems and leaves.

**6** Cut two 20-hole x 64-hole pieces

for birdhouse sides. Beginning 24 holes from the top, free-form stitch the sides, following similar pattern used for black, maroon and red Straight Stitches on front and back. Unworked areas on sides will be covered by roof.

## Birdhouse Assembly

**1** With wrong sides facing and using black, Whipstitch together short ends of sides that are adjacent to unstitched areas.

**2** Beginning at top, Whipstitch sides to front with black, easing around curves as needed to fit. Whipstitch remaining short ends of sides together with red.

**3** For bird perch, push dowel halfway into hole on front; glue in place. Slip painted plastic canvas ring over dowel and glue in place.

**4** Whipstitch back to sides following instructions in step 2.

**5** Glue one rectangular window to front on each side of perch. Glue round window to front under roof peak. Glue remaining rectangular windows to back, placing in same locations as the three windows on front.

## Roof

**1** Cut roof pieces following graph.

**2** Continental Stitch roof pieces

with gray. When background stitching is completed, work black Straight Stitches for shingles following graph or Straight Stitch shingles as desired.

**3** Whipstitch top edges of roof pieces together with gray; Overcast remaining edges with white.

**4** Glue roof to top of barn. If desired, glue only one side to top of barn so birdhouse can be used for storage or a bank, cutting a hole in unstitched area under roof. #

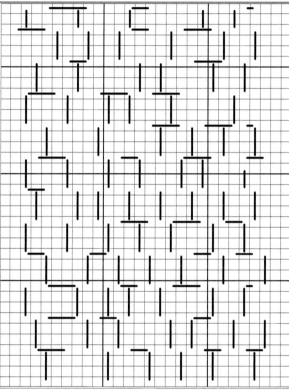

**Roof**
28 holes x 36 holes
Cut 2

**Rectangular Window**
6 holes x 8 holes
Cut 5

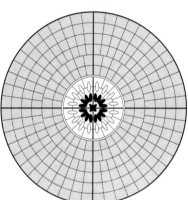

**Round Window**
Cut 1 from radial circle,
cutting away gray area

| COLOR KEY | |
|---|---|
| **Worsted Weight Yarn** | **Yards** |
| Red | 40 |
| ■ Black | 26 |
| Maroon | 14 |
| □ White | 10 |
| Uncoded areas on roof are gray Continental Stitches | 32 |
| ⁄ Gray Whipstitching | |
| ⁄ Black Straight Stitch | |
| Green Straight Stitch | 4 |
| Yellow French Knot | 6 |

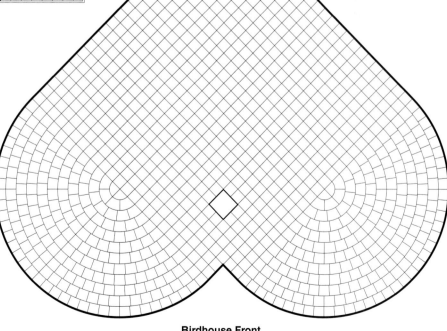

Top

**Birdhouse Front**
Cut 1

# Diamond Princess Photo Frame

Design by Janna Britton

*Show your pride in your precious little one by stitching this enchanting, flower-bedecked frame!*

## Skill level • Beginner

## Finished Size

6¾ inches W x 5½ inches H, including bow

## Materials

- ½ sheet 10-count plastic canvas
- DMC 6-strand embroidery floss as listed in color key
- #16 tapestry needle
- 18 inches 1⅝-inch-wide baby blue sheer organza ribbon
- 3¾-inch x 4⅜-inch piece paper backing in coordinating color
- Transparent tape (optional)
- 4-inch strip magnet
- Low-temperature glue gun

## Project Note

To provide fuller coverage, always work with 12 plies floss, separating strands after threading needle.

## Instructions

**1** Cut plastic canvas according to graphs.

**2** Stitch and Overcast pieces following graphs, working uncoded areas with light violet Continental Stitches.

**3** For bow, pinch ribbon in center to gather, then make two loops on each side; bring tails down. Cut an inverted "V" in tail ends. Tie bow in center with pale delft blue floss and tack to center top of frame.

**4** Using photo as a guide, tack large rose to center of bow, gluing leaves behind top corners of rose.

**5** Tack rosebuds through ribbon tails to frame with long strands forest green floss, threading through hole indicated with green dot on each rosebud graph and working slightly loose Straight Stitches as desired near rosebuds for leaves. Secure floss as desired behind large rose.

**6** Glue paper backing to backside of frame around side and bottom edges. Insert photo through opening in top, holding in place with a bit of tape if necessary.

**7** Cut magnet strip in half; glue strips to back of project at top and bottom. #

**Leaf A**
5 holes x 6 holes
Cut 1

**Leaf B**
4 holes x 7 holes
Cut 1

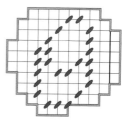

**Large Rose**
11 holes x 10 holes
Cut 1

**Rosebud A**
4 holes x 5 holes
Cut 1

**Rosebud B**
5 holes x 5 holes
Cut 1

**COLOR KEY**

| 6-Strand Embroidery Floss | Yards |
|---|---|
| ☐ Very light violet #153 | 9 |
| ■ Medium violet #552 | 2 |
| ☐ Pale delft blue #800 | 16 |
| ☐ Forest green #989 | 2 |
| Uncoded area are light violet #554 Continental Stitches | 5 |
| ✎ Light violet #554 Overcasting | |

Color numbers given are for DMC 6-strand embroidery floss.

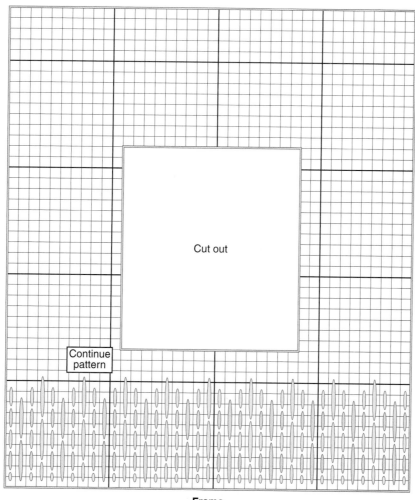

Cut out

Continue pattern

**Frame**
39 holes x 45 holes
Cut 1

# Victorian Cracker Cottage

*Design by Janelle Giese*

Gingerbread trims and delicate details make this elegant house the perfect container for your finest gourmet snacks!

## Skill level • Advanced

## Finished Size

6¼ inches W x 13⅞ inches H x 6 inches D

## Materials

- 2 artist-size sheets stiff 7-count plastic canvas
- Coats & Clark Red Heart Classic worsted weight yarn Art. E267 as listed in color key
- Kreinik Heavy (#32) Braid as listed in color key
- DMC #3 pearl cotton as listed in color key
- DMC #5 pearl cotton as listed in color key
- #16 tapestry needle
- Small amount pale yellow 6-strand embroidery floss
- Mill Hill Products ceramic cottage flower pot button #86081 from Gay Bowles Sales Inc.
- Thick white glue

## Cutting

**1** Cut plastic canvas according to graphs (pages 62–66).

**2** Cut one 2-hole x 32-hole piece for step tread and one 30-hole x 39-hole piece for cottage base. Base will remain unstitched.

## Walls

**1** Stitch front, back and side walls following graphs, working uncoded areas on all windowpanes with pale blue Continental Stitches. Do not stitch blue highlighted areas and Whipstitch bars highlighted with red, blue and yellow at this time.

**2** When background stitching is completed, work heavy braid Straight Stitches on windowpanes, working a set of two vertical stitches on top windows where indicated.

**3** Work dark beaver gray pearl cotton Straight Stitches and Backstitches on windows, placing one vertical stitch between each set of vertical braid stitches.

**4** Use a full strand honey gold to work Cross Stitch over door handle. Work remaining embroidery with black #3 and #5 pearl cotton following graphs.

## Porch

**1** Stitch porch, porch roof, porch front, posts and step risers following graphs, working uncoded areas on porch roof with Windsor blue Continental Stitches. Do not work blue highlighted Whipstitch bar at this time.

**2** Continental Stitch and Overcast step tread with nickel.

## Cottage Assembly

**1** Whipstitch front to side walls, using Continental Stitches as indicated on red highlighted lines, then complete the pattern stitches on side walls in blue highlighted areas.

**2** Overcast top edges of walls with bronze. Using nickel, Overcast porch areas on left and right walls that are not in brackets. Do not overcast bottom edges.

**3** Whipstitch two posts together along a side edge. Repeat with remaining two posts, so there are two sets of posts.

**4** Whipstitch one set to back of post on right side and one to back of post of left side, using Continental Stitches to Whipstitch portion inside brackets to side walls along yellow highlighted line nearest cottage.

**5** Whipstitch porch front to posts and to side walls, using Continental Stitches to Whipstitch portion inside brackets to side walls along remaining yellow highlighted line. Overcast bottom edge of trim on front between posts.

**Continued on page 62**

**6** Overcast all edges outside the bracket on porch roof. Whipstitch portion inside bracket to bar highlighted with blue on front wall. Using Continental Stitches, Whipstitch bar highlighted with blue on porch roof to top edge of porch front.

**7** Overcast top edge of one step riser, then Whipstitch ends of this riser to bottom step between brackets. Overcast top and bottom edges of remaining riser, then Whipstitch ends to top step between brackets.

**8** Using eggshell, Overcast all edges outside the bracket on porch. Whipstitch portion inside bracket to bar highlighted with red on front wall. Use pale yellow embroidery floss to Whipstitch ceramic button to front wall as in photo.

**9** Using dark sage, Whipstitch unstitched base to bottom edges of walls and to bottom step riser. Glue porch to top step riser. Center and glue step tread in place on bottom step.

## Gables & Soffits

**1** For each gable and each soffit, place one backing/insert piece behind one face, matching top edges, then stitch as one following face graph. Pink highlighted areas on gable faces and green highlighted lines and area below them on gables and soffits will remain unstitched.

**2** Whipstitch top edges of each gable face and backing together where indicated with bronze.

## Roof, Cornice & Gingerbread Facing

**1** Stitch gingerbread facing and both roof pieces following graphs, leaving area not coded on roof pieces unworked at this time.

**2** Overcast outside edges of cornice with eggshell. Overcast inside edges of gingerbread facing and edges around sides and bottom from dot to dot. Work Straight Stitches over opening, when Overcasting is completed.

## Roof Assembly

**1** Using Continental Stitches indicated, Whipstitch side edges of soffits to gable faces along blue highlighted lines, then complete cornmeal pattern stitches on gables in pink areas. Overcast extended

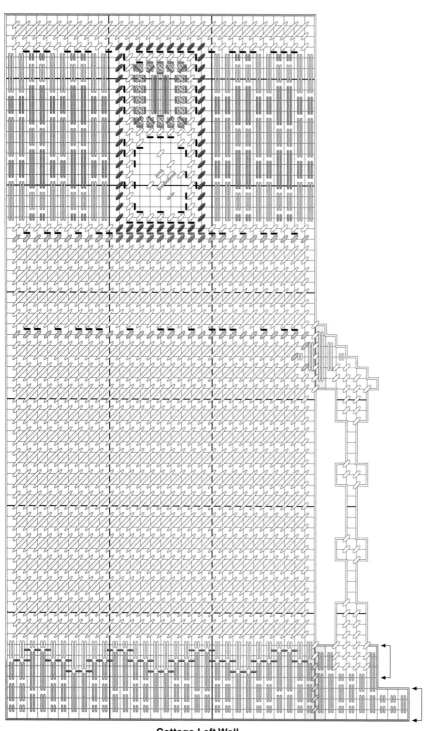

**Cottage Left Wall**
39 holes x 66 holes
Cut 1

edges of gables with Windsor blue.

**2** Using country blue, Whipstitch top edges of soffits to bar on roof pieces highlighted with blue. **Note:** *Edges of roof will extend four holes at front and three holes at back.* Whipstitch top edges of roof pieces together with country blue.

**3** Following pattern, fill in remaining unworked areas on roof pieces, working over Whipstitch bars.

**4** Using Windsor blue, Whipstitch gingerbread facing to front edge of roof; Overcast remaining edges of roof.

**5** Using eggshell throughout, slide cornice up over gables and soffits to highlighted green Whipstitch lines, then Whipstitch together. Whipstitch together unworked corners of gables and soffits (lid insert); Overcast bottom edges. #

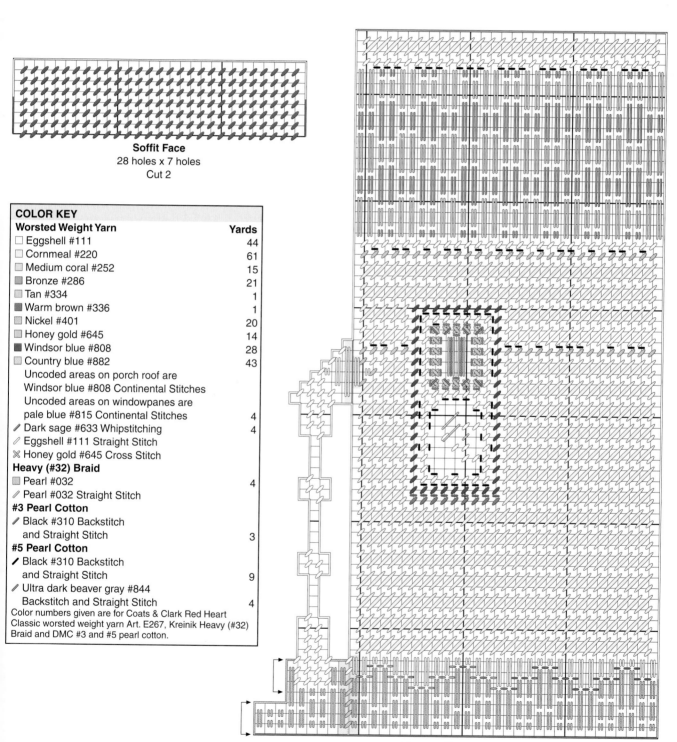

**Soffit Face**
28 holes x 7 holes
Cut 2

**COLOR KEY**

| Worsted Weight Yarn | Yards |
|---|---|
| ☐ Eggshell #111 | 44 |
| ☐ Cornmeal #220 | 61 |
| ☐ Medium coral #252 | 15 |
| ■ Bronze #286 | 21 |
| ☐ Tan #334 | 1 |
| ■ Warm brown #336 | 1 |
| ☐ Nickel #401 | 20 |
| ☐ Honey gold #645 | 14 |
| ■ Windsor blue #808 | 28 |
| ☐ Country blue #882 | 43 |
| Uncoded areas on porch roof are | |
| Windsor blue #808 Continental Stitches | |
| Uncoded areas on windowpanes are | |
| pale blue #815 Continental Stitches | 4 |
| ╱ Dark sage #633 Whipstitching | 4 |
| ╱ Eggshell #111 Straight Stitch | |
| ✕ Honey gold #645 Cross Stitch | |
| **Heavy (#32) Braid** | |
| ☐ Pearl #032 | 4 |
| ╱ Pearl #032 Straight Stitch | |
| **#3 Pearl Cotton** | |
| ╱ Black #310 Backstitch | |
| and Straight Stitch | 3 |
| **#5 Pearl Cotton** | |
| ╱ Black #310 Backstitch | |
| and Straight Stitch | 9 |
| ╱ Ultra dark beaver gray #844 | |
| Backstitch and Straight Stitch | 4 |

Color numbers given are for Coats & Clark Red Heart Classic worsted weight yarn Art. E267, Kreinik Heavy (#32) Braid and DMC #3 and #5 pearl cotton.

**Cottage Right Wall**
39 holes x 66 holes
Cut 1

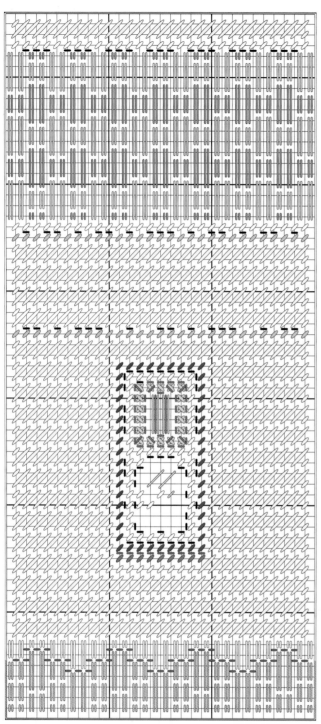

**Cottage Back Wall**
30 holes x 66 holes
Cut 1

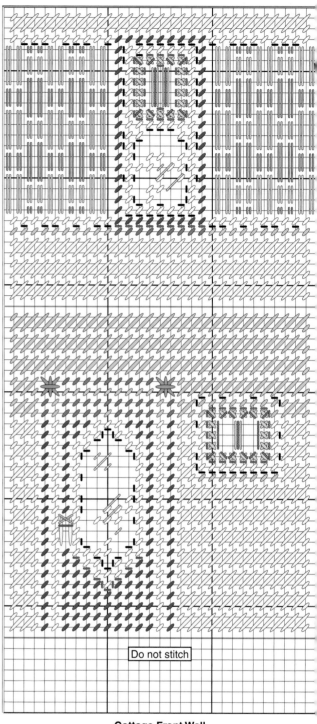

Do not stitch

**Cottage Front Wall**
30 holes x 66 holes
Cut 1

**Step Riser**
30 holes x 3 holes
Cut 2

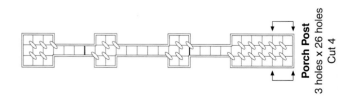

**Porch Post**
3 holes x 26 holes
Cut 4

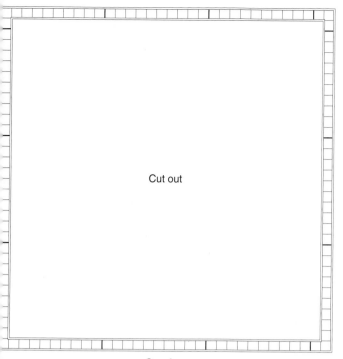

**Cornice**
32 holes x 32 holes
Cut 1

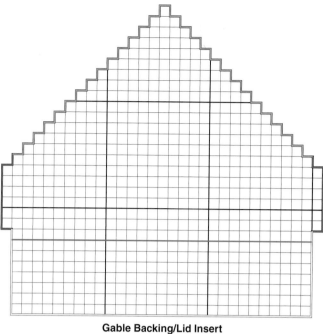

**Gable Backing/Lid Insert**
31 holes x 29 holes
Cut 2

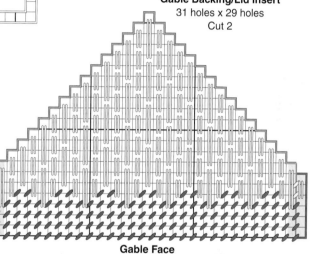

**Gable Face**
31 holes x 21 holes
Cut 2

**COLOR KEY**

| Worsted Weight Yarn | Yards |
|---|---|
| ☐ Eggshell #111 | 44 |
| ☐ Cornmeal #220 | 61 |
| ☐ Medium coral #252 | 15 |
| ☐ Bronze #286 | 21 |
| ☐ Tan #334 | 1 |
| ☐ Warm brown #336 | 1 |
| ☐ Nickel #401 | 20 |
| ☐ Honey gold #645 | 14 |
| ☐ Windsor blue #808 | 28 |
| ☐ Country blue #882 | 43 |
| Uncoded areas on porch roof are | |
| Windsor blue #808 Continental Stitches | |
| Uncoded areas on windowpanes are | |
| pale blue #815 Continental Stitches | 4 |
| ∕ Dark sage #633 Whipstitching | 4 |
| ∕ Eggshell #111 Straight Stitch | |
| ✕ Honey gold #645 Cross Stitch | |
| **Heavy (#32) Braid** | |
| ☐ Pearl #032 | 4 |
| ∕ Pearl #032 Straight Stitch | |
| **#3 Pearl Cotton** | |
| ∕ Black #310 Backstitch | |
| and Straight Stitch | 3 |
| **#5 Pearl Cotton** | |
| ∕ Black #310 Backstitch | |
| and Straight Stitch | 9 |
| ∕ Ultra dark beaver gray #844 | |
| Backstitch and Straight Stitch | 4 |

Color numbers given are for Coats & Clark Red Heart
Classic worsted weight yarn Art. E267, Kreinik Heavy (#32)
Braid and DMC #3 and #5 pearl cotton.

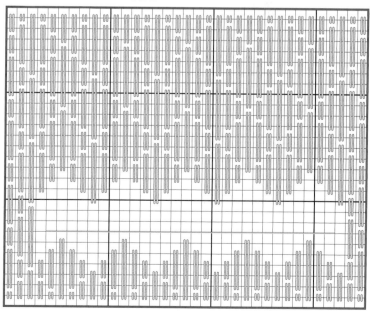

**Cottage Roof**
35 holes x 28 holes
Cut 2

Whipstitch to bar highlighted with blue on porch roof

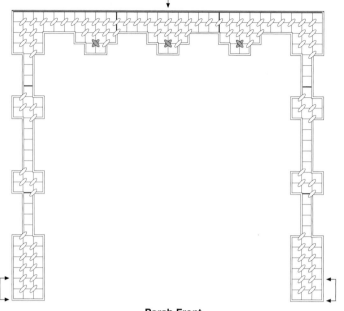

**Porch Front**
30 holes x 27 holes
Cut 1

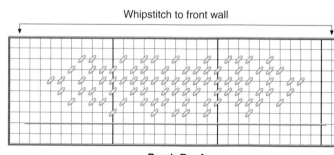

**Soffit Backing/Lid Insert**
28 holes x 15 holes
Cut 2

**Porch**
32 holes x 7 holes
Cut 1

Whipstitch to front wall

**Porch Roof**
32 holes x 10 holes
Cut 1

| COLOR KEY | |
|---|---|
| **Worsted Weight Yarn** | **Yards** |
| ☐ Eggshell #111 | 44 |
| ☐ Cornmeal #220 | 61 |
| ☐ Medium coral #252 | 15 |
| ■ Bronze #286 | 21 |
| ☐ Tan #334 | 1 |
| ■ Warm brown #336 | 1 |
| ☐ Nickel #401 | 20 |
| ☐ Honey gold #645 | 14 |
| ■ Windsor blue #808 | 28 |
| ☐ Country blue #882 | 43 |
| Uncoded areas on porch roof are Windsor blue #808 Continental Stitches | |
| Uncoded areas on windowpanes are pale blue #815 Continental Stitches | 4 |
| ╱ Dark sage #633 Whipstitching | 4 |
| ╱ Eggshell #111 Straight Stitch | |
| ✕ Honey gold #645 Cross Stitch | |
| **Heavy (#32) Braid** | |
| ☐ Pearl #032 | 4 |
| ╱ Pearl #032 Straight Stitch | |
| **#3 Pearl Cotton** | |
| ╱ Black #310 Backstitch and Straight Stitch | 3 |
| **#5 Pearl Cotton** | |
| ╱ Black #310 Backstitch and Straight Stitch | 9 |
| ╱ Ultra dark beaver gray #844 Backstitch and Straight Stitch | 4 |

Color numbers given are for Coats & Clark Red Heart Classic worsted weight yarn Art. E267, Kreinik Heavy (#32) Braid and DMC #3 and #5 pearl cotton.

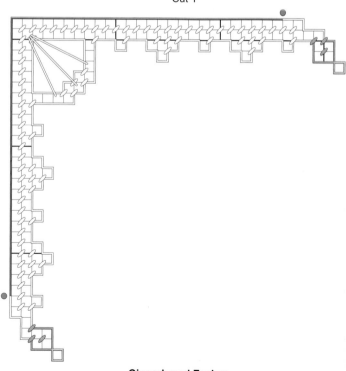

**Gingerbread Facing**
32 holes x 32 holes
Cut 1

# A Bit of Ireland Treasure Box

Design by Mary T. Cosgrove

May the luck o' the Irish bring you plenty of treasures to store inside this beautiful box!

## Skill level • Intermediate

### Finished Size

4¼ inches square

### Materials

- 1 sheet almond Uniek QuickCount 7-count plastic canvas
- 1 sheet dusty rose Uniek QuickCount 7-count plastic canvas
- Uniek Needloft plastic canvas yarn as listed in color key
- #16 tapestry needle
- 6 inches gold metallic braid or cord

### Instructions

**1** Cut plastic canvas according to graphs (page 73). Cut four 24-hole x 3-hole pieces each from almond and dusty rose plastic canvas for lid rims. All lid rims and all dusty rose pieces will remain unstitched.

**2** Stitch almond top, bottom and sides following graphs.

**3** Using forest through step 6, place one almond rim and one dusty rose rim together, then Whipstitch together along bottom edges. Repeat with remaining rims.

**4** With almond on the outside, whipstitch side edges of rims together, forming a square. Whipstitch top edges of rims to unstitched dusty rose top along blue highlighted bars. Whipstitch wrong sides of dusty rose and almond top pieces together along outside edges.

**5** To line sides and bottom, place one unstitched dusty rose piece on wrong side of corresponding stitched piece.

**6** For each side, Whipstitch top edges of dusty rose and almond piece together, then Whipstitch sides together; Whipstitch sides to bottom.

**7** Attach gold metallic braid or cord to a center bottom hole of a lid rim with a Lark's Head Knot. Keeping knot on the inside, bring loop to outside when placing lid on box. #

# Secret Dreams Journal Cover

Design by Kristine Loffredo

With its soft, feminine colors and graceful stitch patterns,
this lovely journal cover is sure to be a favorite of both mom and daughter!

## Skill level • Intermediate

## Finished Size

5⅞ inches W x 8¾ inches H x
¾ inch D; fits 5½-inch x
8½-inch journal

## Materials

- 1½ sheets 7-count plastic canvas
- Uniek Needloft plastic canvas yarn as listed in color key
- Uniek Needloft iridescent craft cord as listed in color key
- #16 tapestry needle
- 2 (8¾-inch) lengths gold metallic rickrack
- Hot-glue gun

## Instructions

**1** Cut and stitch plastic canvas according to graphs.

**2** Using bright purple through step 3, Whipstitch cover edges indicated to long spine edges.

**3** Overcast one long edge of each pocket. With wrong sides together, Whipstitch remaining edges of pockets to cover edges, Overcasting remaining cover and spine edges while Whipstitching.

Glue rickrack where
indicated on cover front and
back, trimming ends so
they do not hang over edges. #

Attach rickrack

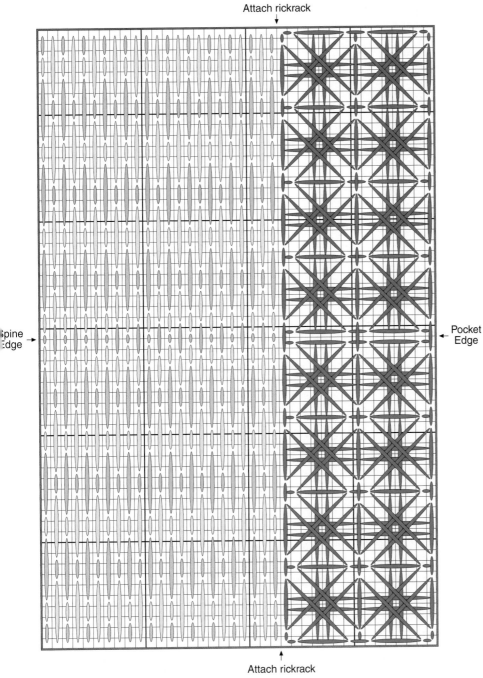

Spine
Edge →

← Pocket
Edge

Attach rickrack

**Journal Cover Front & Back**
38 holes x 58 holes
Cut 2

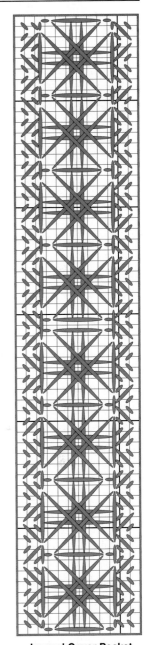

**Journal Cover Pocket**
12 holes x 58 holes
Cut 2

**Journal Cover Spine**
4 holes x 58 holes
Cut 1

# Elegant Monogram Checkbook Cover

Design by Kathy Wirth

Put some sparkle in your life with this personalized checkbook cover. It's the perfect accessory for a fun-filled shopping spree!

## Skill level • Intermediate

## Finished Size

6⅝ inches W x 3⅝ inches L x ⅝ inches D

## Materials

- 1 sheet black 10-count plastic canvas
- Kreinik ¹⁄₁₆-inch-wide metallic ribbon as listed in color key
- #3 pearl cotton as listed in color key
- #22 tapestry needle
- #24 tapestry needle

## Project Notes

Use #22 needle with pearl cotton and #24 needle with metallic ribbon.

To easily thread needles, fold a small piece of paper over ribbon end and pass through eye.

## Instructions

**1** Cut plastic canvas according to graphs. Do not stitch one each of front, back and spine which will be used as liners. Pocket pieces will also remain unstitched.

**2** Stitch remaining front, back and spine following graphs, keeping stitches smooth and flat. Using alphabet given and graph as a sample, work desired initials in center of diamond shapes on front, filling in with black ribbon Straight Stitches.

**3** Using black pearl cotton through step 4, hold stitched pieces and unworked liners together, then Whipstitch spine to front and back along long edges.

**4** Matching bottom edges, place unworked pockets next to lining on front and back, Whipstitching remaining outside edges of stitched pieces and liners together while attaching pockets. #

| COLOR KEY | |
|---|---|
| **¹⁄₁₆-Inch-Wide Metallic Ribbon** | **Yards** |
| ☐ Silver hi lustre #001HL | 14 |
| ☐ Black #005 | 3 |
| ■ Purple #012 | 15 |
| ☐ Chartreuse #015 | 9 |
| **#3 Pearl Cotton** | |
| ✐ Black Whipstitching | 9 |
| Color numbers given are for Kreinik ¹⁄₁₆-inch wide metallic ribbon. | |

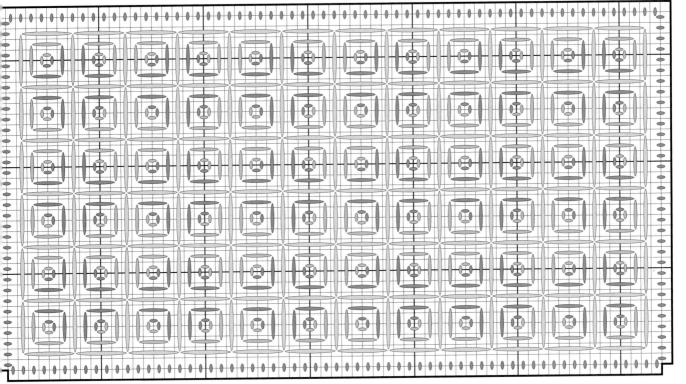

**Checkbook Cover Back**
65 holes x 35 holes
Cut 2, stitch 1

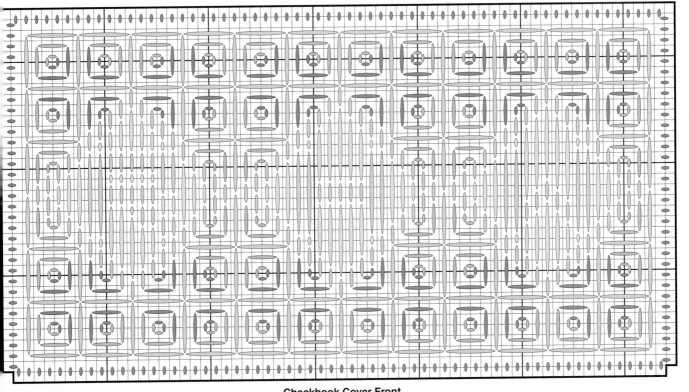

**Checkbook Cover Front**
65 holes x 35 holes
Cut 2, stitch 1

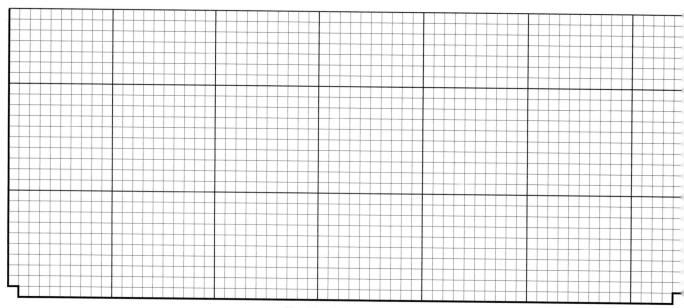

**Checkbook Cover Pocket**
65 holes x 27 holes
Cut 2
Do not stitch

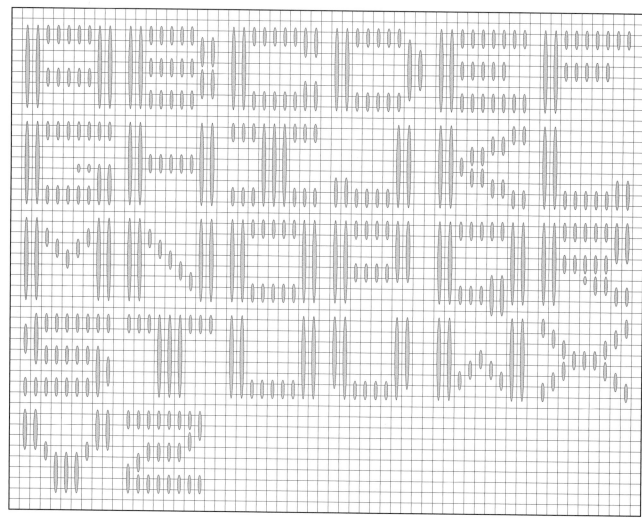

**Checkbook Cover Alphabet**

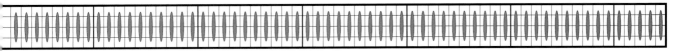

**Checkbook Cover Spine**
65 holes x 4 holes
Cut 2, stitch 1

| COLOR KEY | |
| --- | --- |
| **1/16-Inch-Wide Metallic Ribbon** | **Yards** |
| ▨ Silver hi lustre #001HL | 14 |
| ☐ Black #005 | 3 |
| ■ Purple #012 | 15 |
| ▨ Chartreuse #015 | 9 |
| **#3 Pearl Cotton** | |
| ✎ Black Whipstitching | 9 |
| Color numbers given are for Kreinik 1/16-inch wide metallic ribbon. | |

A Bit of Ireland Treasure Box continued from page 67

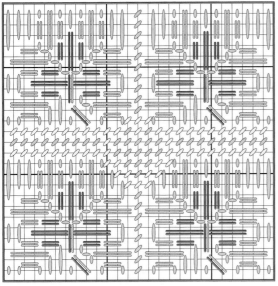

**Box Side**
26 holes x 26 holes
Cut 4 from almond
Stitch as graphed
Cut 4 from dusty rose
Do not stitch

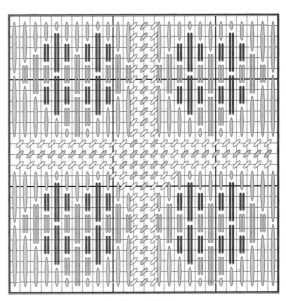

**Box Top & Bottom**
26 holes x 26 holes
Cut 2 from almond
Stitch as graphed
Cut 2 from dusty rose
Do not stitch

| COLOR KEY | |
| --- | --- |
| **Plastic Canvas Yarn** | **Yards** |
| ▨ Lavender #05 | 23 |
| ▨ Moss #25 | 22 |
| ■ Forest #29 | 25 |
| ☐ Eggshell #39 | 8 |
| Color numbers given are for Uniek Needloft plastic canvas yarn. | |

# CHAPTER FOUR

# Long Stitch

Cover large areas quickly and easily by using Long Stitches!

Welcome to the wonderful world of Long Stitches, where the longer design lines lend themselves to fine geometrics and graceful curves!

**Long Stitch**

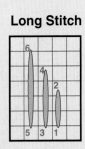

Our selection of delightful designs includes plenty of eye-catching projects, ranging from the quietly elegant to the fun and fanciful!

# Interwoven Doily

Design by Kathy Wirth

The handsome colors and fascinating
interlocked pattern of this unique doily
make it the perfect accent
for the den or study!

| COLOR KEY | |
|---|---|
| **#3 Pearl Cotton** | **Yards** |
| ☐ Very light ecru #926 | 38 |
| ■ Medium dark raspberry #1028 | 38 |
| Uncoded areas are medium dark raspberry #1028 Continental Stitches | |
| **¹⁄₈-Inch Metallic Needlepoint Yarn** | |
| ☐ Gold #PC1 | 15 |
| Color numbers given are for Coats & Clark Anchor #3 pearl cotton and Rainbow Gallery Plastic Canvas 7 Metallic Needlepoint Yarn. | |

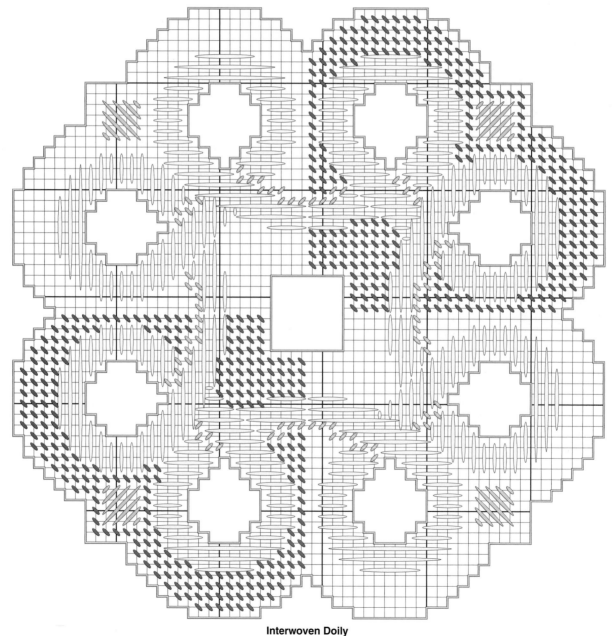

**Interwoven Doily**
57 holes x 57 holes
Cut 2, stitch 1

# Floral Impressions Coaster Set

Design by Janelle Giese

Upturned leaves and daintily scalloped edgings give this jewel-toned coaster set an air of delicate poise!

## Skill Level • Intermediate

### Finished Size

**Coasters:** 4¾ inches W x 4¾ inches H

**Holder:** 4⅜ inches W x 3 inches H x 1⅜ inches D

## Materials

- 2 sheets black 7-count plastic canvas
- Uniek Needloft plastic canvas yarn as listed in color key
- Kreinik Heavy (#32) Braid as listed in color key
- #5 pearl cotton as listed in color key
- #16 tapestry needle

### Project Note

Since stitches are heavy and coasters small, it may be easier to stitch fronts on a large piece of canvas, then cut out before Whipstitching to backs.

### Cutting

**1** Cut plastic canvas according to graphs (page 78).

**2** Cut two 7-hole x 9-hole pieces for holder sides and one 2-hole x 7-hole piece for holder base. Sides and base will remain unstitched.

### Coasters

**1** Using a double strand plastic canvas yarn, stitch coaster fronts following graph, keeping stitches smooth and flat. Using heavy braid, work stitches in center of each coaster, using two strands per stitch where indicated.

**2** When background stitching is completed, Backstitch around bright pink yarn with heavy braid.

**3** Whipstitch one coaster back to each front with black.

### Holder

**1** Continental Stitch one each of holder front and back, leaving red highlighted Whipstitch lines on front unworked at this time.

**2** Using black pearl cotton, work embroidery on holder front and back.

**3** Place stitched holder front on corresponding unstitched piece and Whipstitch together, leaving bottom edge between arrows unworked at this time.

**4** Place stitched holder back on corresponding unstitched piece and Whipstitch together around sides and top from arrow to arrow.

**5** Using black, Whipstitch one 7-hole edge of each side to 7-hole edges of bottom.

**6** Using mermaid and Continental Stitches, Whipstitch sides to front along red Whipstitch lines. *Note: You will need to double a couple of the stitches to join all the holes on the side to the front. Whipstitch bottom edges between arrows on front to base.*

**7** Using black, Whipstitch sides and base to back, Whipstitching remaining edges of back and liner together at the same time. #

Interwoven Doily continued from page 76

## Finished Size

8½ inches W x 8½ inches L

## Materials

- 2 sheets stiff 7-count plastic canvas
- Coats & Clark Anchor #3 pearl cotton as listed in color key
- ⅛-inch-wide Plastic Canvas 7 Metallic Needlepoint Yarn by Rainbow Gallery as listed in color key
- #16 tapestry needle
- #22 tapestry needle
- 9-inch x 12-inch sheet white self-adhesive Presto Felt by Kunin felt

## Project Notes

Keep pearl cotton and metallic needlepoint yarn smooth and flat while stitching.

Use #16 tapestry needle with pearl cotton and #22 tapestry needle with metallic needlepoint yarn.

## Instructions

**1** Cut plastic canvas according to graph (page 76), cutting out holes on both front and back. Back will remain unstitched.

**2** Using two strands medium dark

raspberry, three strands very light ecru and a single strand gold, stitch front following graph, working uncoded areas with medium dark raspberry Continental Stitches.

**3** Using unstitched back as pattern and including cutout areas, trace outline on paper side of felt. Cut felt approximately ¹⁄₁₆-inch inside lines.

**4** Using gold, Whipstitch front and back together along inside and outside edges.

**5** Adhere felt to unstitched back. #

Floral Impressions Coaster Set continued from page 77

| COLOR KEY | |
|---|---|
| **Plastic Canvas Yarn** | **Yards** |
| ■ Black #00 | 24 |
| ■ Holly #27 | 2 |
| ■ Royal #32 | 6 |
| □ Mermaid #53 | 7 |
| ▨ Bright pink #62 | 11 |
| ■ Bright purple #64 | 8 |
| **Heavy (#32) Braid** | |
| □ Magenta blue #664 | 7 |
| ⁄ Magenta blue #664 Backstitch | |
| **#5 Pearl Cotton** | |
| ⁄ Black Backstitch and Straight Stitch | 1 |
| Color numbers given are for Uniek Needloft plastic canvas yarn and Kreinik Heavy (#32) Braid. | |

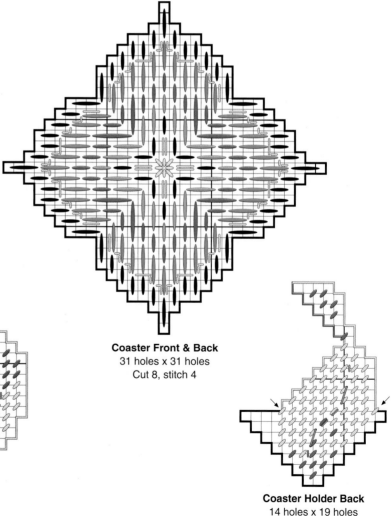

**Coaster Front & Back**
31 holes x 31 holes
Cut 8, stitch 4

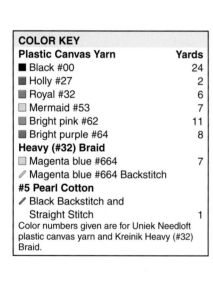

**Coaster Holder Front**
28 holes x 14 holes
Cut 2, stitch 1

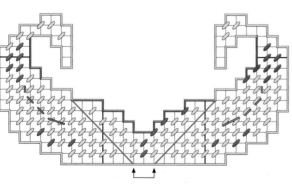

**Coaster Holder Back**
14 holes x 19 holes
Cut 2, stitch 1

# Happy Dreams Tissue Box Cover

Design by Kathy Wirth

*The dreamer in you will wish upon a star as you stitch this lighthearted tissue topper!*

## Skill Level • Beginner

### Finished Size

Fits boutique-style tissue box

## Materials

- 2 sheets 10-count plastic canvas
- Coats & Clark Red Heart Classic worsted weight yarn Art. E267 as listed in color key
- Coats & Clark Red Heart Kids worsted weight yarn Art. E711 as listed in color key
- #20 tapestry needle
- Permanent black marker
- Hot-glue gun

### Instructions

**1** Cut plastic canvas according to graphs (pages 80 and 81).

**2** Mark position of mouth and eyes on stars and moon with black permanent marker, then using 1 yard lengths, stitch pieces following graphs, working dark colors last and leaving uncoded areas on sides unstitched.

**3** Overcast stars and moons with yellow, using black to Overcast mouth edges on moon. Using pale blue, Overcast inside edges of top, and bottom edges of sides; Whipstitch sides together, then Whipstitch sides to top.

**4** Glue shapes to unstitched areas on sides. #

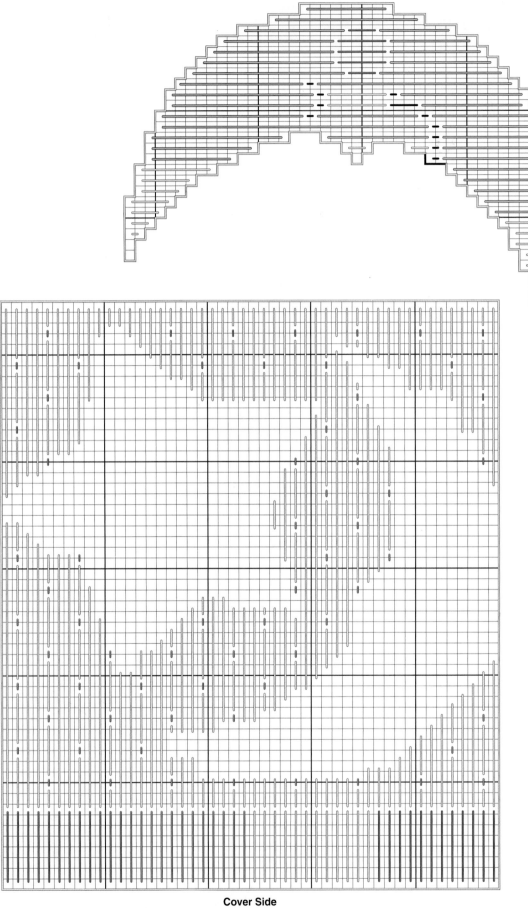

**Moon**
30 holes x 43 holes
Cut 4

**Cover Side**
48 holes x 55 holes
Cut 4

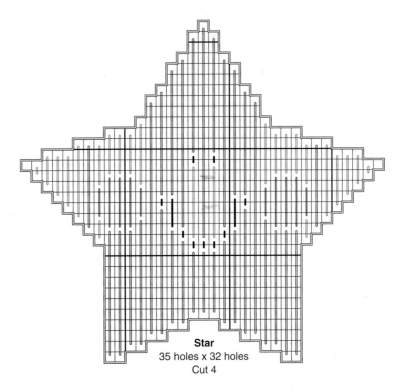

**COLOR KEY**

| Worsted Weight Yarn | Yards |
|---|---|
| ■ Black #12 | 2 |
| □ Yellow #230 | 34 |
| □ Pale blue #815 | 50 |
| ■ Red #2390 | 7 |
| ■ Green #2677 | 5 |
| ■ Blue #2845 | 17 |

Color numbers given are for Coats & Clark Red Heart Classic worsted weight yarn Art. E267 and Kids worsted weight yarn Art. E711.

**Star**
35 holes x 32 holes
Cut 4

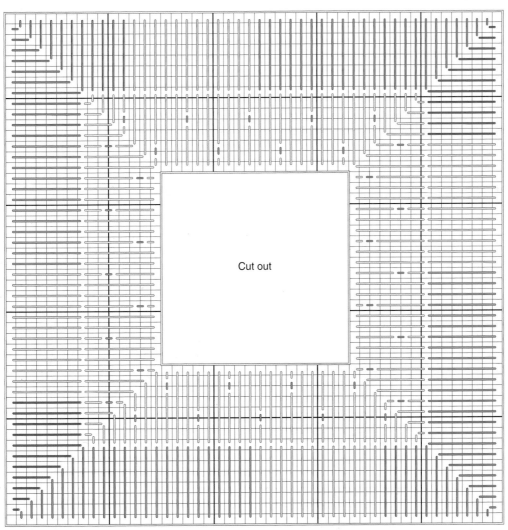

Cut out

**Cover Top**
48 holes x 48 holes
Cut 1

# Frosty Starcatcher

Design by Janelle Giese

Catch the sparkle of the winter stars with a sweep of Frosty's broom.
You'll love the way this fanciful accent brightens up your indoor mood!

## Skill Level • Advanced

## Finished Size

8⅝ inches W x 16 inches H, excluding hanger

## Materials

- ⅔ sheet stiff 7-count plastic canvas
- Uniek Needloft plastic canvas yarn as listed in color key
- #5 pearl cotton as listed in color key
- Kreinik Medium (#16) Braid as listed in color key
- Kreinik Heavy (#32) Braid as listed in color key
- #16 tapestry needle
- 28 (7mm) silver jump rings
- 14 (7mm) clear round rhinestones
- 7 (25mm) crystal transparent starflake beads
- 6 (18mm) crystal transparent starflake beads
- 18-inch-long silver necklace chain
- Needle-nose pliers with cutters
- Thick white glue

## Instructions

1 Cut plastic canvas according to graph (page 84).

2 Stitch piece following graph, working uncoded areas in lavender shaded areas with moonstone Cross Stitches and uncoded background on pompom and under pearl Straight Stitches on snowman with white Continental Stitches. Work two stitches per hole on hat, scarf and broom as shown.

3 Overcast coded edges, leaving scarf edges unworked where indicated.

4 When background stitching is completed, use pearl to work Straight Stitches over white and baby blue Continental Stitches on snowman.

5 Stitch eyes with full strand black yarn, then work eye with a black pearl cotton Straight Stitch on each side of black yarn stitch. Stitch eye highlights with pearl, splitting center of black yarn stitch.

6 Use 1 ply camel to work embroidery on broom bristles. Use amethyst for embroidery on moon. Use moonstone to work embroidery on center of hatband, wrapping braid around needle one time for French Knots.

7 Work all remaining embroidery with black pearl cotton.

8 For scarf fringe, cut eight 3-inch lengths of white yarn. Attach lengths with a Lark's Head Knot where indicated at ends of scarf. Trim yarn ends to ¾ inch beyond knots.

## Finishing

1 Cut 13 (1-inch) lengths from silver necklace chain. Remaining 5-inch length will be used for hanging.

2 Attach one jump ring to each end of each chain length. For hanger, attach a jump ring on 5-inch length to top of starcatcher where indicated with arrow.

3 To make starflake chains, use jump rings to attach ends of each chain to a starflake bead, following steps 4 and 5.

4 For center chain: attach bottom jump ring on top length to large bead. Attach top ring of second chain to same large bead, then attach bottom ring to small bead. Continue attaching beads in following order: large, small, large.

5 For each side chain, follow instructions in step 4 and attach in following order: small, large, small, large.

6 Place completed chains on a flat surface and glue one rhinestone to center of each large bead. Allow to dry. Turn chains over and glue remaining rhinestones to other sides of large beads.

7 Attach top jump ring of each chain to bottom of starcatcher where indicated with arrows. #

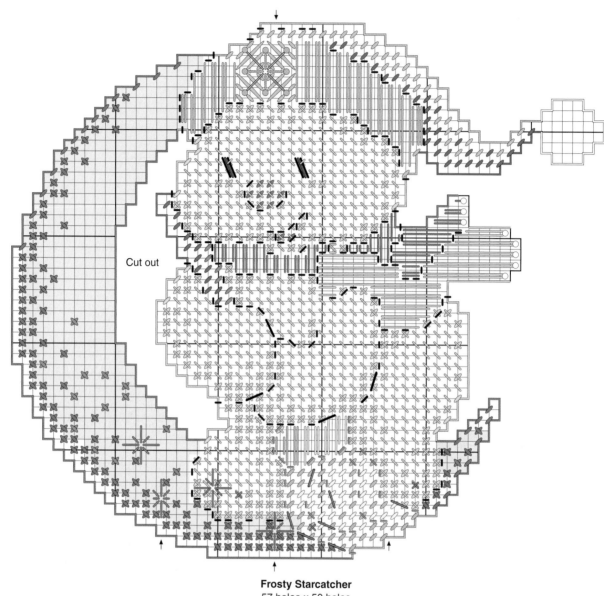

**Frosty Starcatcher**
57 holes x 50 holes
Cut 1

Cut out

| COLOR KEY | | | |
|---|---|---|---|
| **Plastic Canvas Yarn** | **Yards** | **Heavy (#32) Braid** | **Yards** |
| ■ Lavender #05 | 2 | ■ Amethyst #026 | 2 |
| ■ Cinnamon #14 | 1 | ■ Ametrine #3223 | 8 |
| ☐ Baby yellow #21 | 1 | Uncoded areas in lavender shaded areas | |
| ■ Moss #25 | 1 | are moonstone #3231 Cross Stitches | 9 |
| ☐ Baby blue #36 | 6 | ∕ Amethyst #026 Straight Stitch | |
| ■ Beige #40 | 2 | ∕ Moonstone #3231 Straight Stitch | |
| ■ Camel #43 | 1 | ● Moonstone #3231 French Knot | |
| ☐ Orchid #44 | 3 | **Medium (#16) Braid** | |
| ■ Bright green #61 | 4 | ∕ Pearl #32 Straight Stitch | 11 |
| Uncoded background on pompom and | | **#5 Pearl Cotton** | |
| under pearl Straight Stitches on snowman | | ∕ Black Backstitch and | |
| are white #41 Continental Stitches | 10 | Straight Stitch | 4 |
| ∕ White #41 Overcasting | | Color numbers given are for Uniek Needloft plastic canvas | |
| ∕ Black #00 Straight Stitch | 1 | yarn and Kreinik Heavy (#32) Braid and Medium (#16) Braid. | |
| ∕ Camel #43 Backstitch | | | |
| and Straight Stitch | | | |
| ○ White #41 Lark's Head Knot | | | |

# Pastel Frame Mini Mirror

Design by Alida Macor

Delicate colors and eye-pleasing design lines make this tiny mirror a natural accent for any room!

## Skill Level • Beginner

## Finished Size

7½ inches square

## Materials

- 1 (12-inch x 18-inch) sheet 7-count plastic canvas
- Uniek Needloft plastic canvas yarn as listed in color key
- #16 tapestry needle
- 4-inch square mirror
- Small sawtooth hanger

## Instructions

**1** Cut plastic canvas according to graph (page 93), cutting out opening for front only. Back will remain unstitched.

**2** Stitch front following graph, leaving stitch areas shaded with blue unworked at this time. Overcast inside edges with fern.

**3** Center sawtooth hanger on back; attach four holes from the top with fern, tying off securely in a knot.

**4** Center mirror between front and back, then work white stitches as shown in blue shaded areas to hold mirror in place; knot stitches on backside.

**5** Whipstitch front and back together with fern. #

# Mock-Woven Basket Set

*Designs by Angie Arickx*

These charming yet practical projects beautifully simulate the
look of carefully woven baskets! Choose the soft-tones basket for a
pastel pick-me-up, or stitch the Southwest basket for a more rugged accent!

## Skill Level • Beginner

## Finished Size

3¼ inches H x 5¼ inches in
diameter, excluding handles

## Materials

- 1 artist-size sheet 7-count plastic
  canvas
- 2 (6-inch) plastic canvas radial circles
- Uniek Needloft plastic canvas as
  listed in color key
- #16 tapestry needle
- Hot-glue gun

## Instructions

**1** Cut plastic canvas according to
graphs. Cut two outermost rows
of holes from each plastic canvas
radial circle for basket bottoms.
Bottoms will remain unstitched.

**2** Stitch pieces following graphs,
overlapping one row of holes on
baskets as indicated. Work camel
Backstitches on soft-tones basket
and cinnamon Backstitches on
Southwest basket first. Work Long
Stitches on baskets using a double
strand where indicated, keeping
stitches smooth and flat.

**3** Work Cross Stitches on handles

when background stitching is
completed.

**4** Using eggshell for soft-tone
basket and sandstone for
Southwest basket, Overcast
handles and top edges of baskets.
Whipstitch one unstitched bottom
to bottom edge of each basket.

**5** For soft-tone basket, glue ends
of handle inside basket on opposite sides.

**6** For Southwest basket, bend
each handle, forming a loop; glue
ends together at a 90 degree
angle. Glue handles inside basket
on opposite sides. #

**COLOR KEY**

| Plastic Canvas Yarn | Yards |
|---|---|
| ■ Burgundy #03 | 14 |
| ▫ Sandstone #16 | 22 |
| ▫ Moss #25 | 10 |
| ▫ Eggshell #39 | 27 |
| ▫ Lilac #45 | 9 |
| ▫ Turquoise #54 | 10 |
| ╱ Cinnamon #14 Backstitch | 13 |
| ╱ Camel #43 Backstitch | 9 |
| ✗ Cinnamon #14 Cross Stitch | |
| ✗ Camel #43 Cross Stitch | |

Color numbers given are for Uniek Needloft plastic canvas yarn.

Overlap

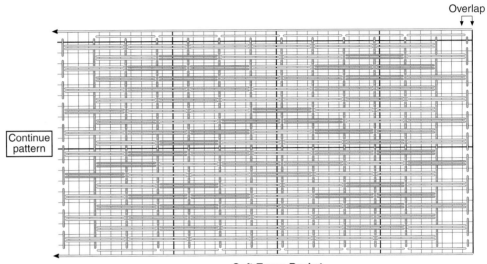

**Soft-Tones Basket**
109 holes x 21 holes
Cut 1

Continue pattern

**Southwest Basket Handle**
43 holes x 3 holes
Cut 2

Overlap

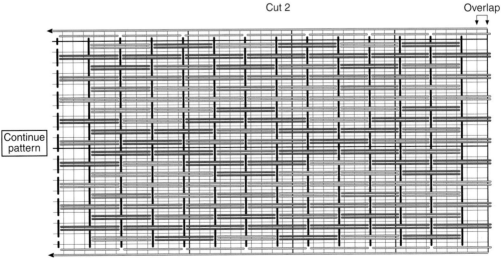

Continue pattern

**Soft-Tones Basket Handle**
3 holes x 71 holes
Cut 1

**Southwest Basket**
109 holes x 21 holes
Cut 1

# Variations on a Theme

*Design by Alida Macor*

You'll love the old-style charm of these exquisite doilies!
Combine the **crispness of white** with the **antique aura of ivory**,
and stitch a set of each for truly versatile decorating!

## Skill Level • Beginner

## Materials

- 1 sheet almond 7-count plastic canvas
- 1 sheet white 7-count plastic canvas
- Uniek Needloft plastic canvas yarn as listed in color key
- Worsted weight yarn as listed in color key
- #16 tapestry needle

## Finished Size

9½ inches W x 9½ inches L

| COLOR KEY | |
| --- | --- |
| **Plastic Canvas Yarn** | **Yards** |
| ☐ Eggshell #39 | 27 |
| **Worsted Weight Yarn** | |
| White | 27 |
| Color number given is for Uniek Needloft plastic canvas yarn. | |

## Instructions

**1** Cut plastic canvas according to graph.

**2** Following graph, stitch and Overcast almond plastic canvas with eggshell; stitch and Overcast white plastic canvas with white. As much as is possible, avoid carrying yarn under unstitched areas. #

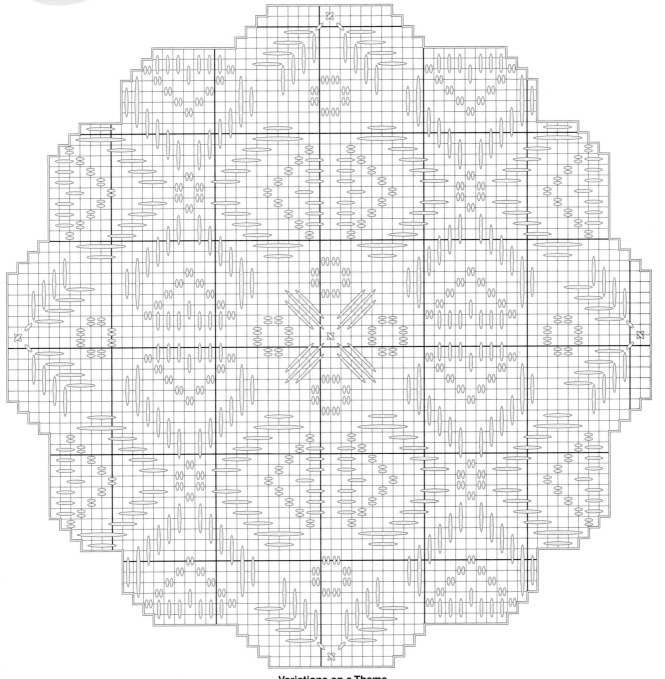

**Variations on a Theme**
62 holes x 62 holes
Cut 1 from almond, stitch as graphed
Cut 1 from white, stitch with white

# Bargello Kitty

Design by Janelle Giese

As lovable as he is soft, this chenille kitty purrs, "Pet me!"
as he adds irresistible appeal to your home decor!

## Skill Level • Advanced

## Finished Size

8¾ inches W x 9 inches H

## Materials

- ⅔ sheet stiff 7-count plastic canvas
- Worsted weight yarn as listed in color key
- Honeysuckle rayon chenille yarn by Elmore-Pisgah Inc. as listed in color key
- #3 pearl cotton as listed in color key
- #5 pearl cotton as listed in color key
- Small amount very light beige brown 6-strand embroidery floss
- #16 tapestry needle
- Sawtooth hanger

## Project Notes

When stitching with worsted weight yarn, use a double strand to work bargello portions of pot and plant, keeping yarn smooth and flat. Use one strand for all other worsted weight stitching.

Use a double strand for all stitching with chenille yarn unless otherwise instructed, keeping yarn smooth and flat.

Place two equal lengths chenille yarn side-by-side, placing nap of yarn in same direction. To make yarn go farther and for better appearance, always stitch with nap. When correcting a mistake, leave yarn in needle and remove in correct stitches by "sewing it out," working stitches in reverse to remove.

## Instructions

**1** Cut plastic canvas according to graph (page 92).

**2** Work Continental Stitches on plant with colors indicated; Overcast leaves with dark blue green. Fill in leaves with bargello pattern in blue greens and light gray.

**3** Work Continental Stitches on pot following graph. Fill in with bargello pattern using terra cottas, browns, light sand and tan. Overcast pot with medium terra cotta.

**4** Work kitty's eyes, ears and nose with worsted weight yarn as graphed. Straight Stitch pupils with a one strand of black yarn.

**5** Stitch and Overcast remaining portions of kitty with chenille yarn, working uncoded areas on muzzle, mouth and paws with ecru Continental Stitches.

**6** Work #3 and #5 pearl cotton Backstitches and Straight Stitches following graph.

**7** Using one strand ecru chenille yarn, Straight Stitch eye highlights and ear tufts.

**8** Using very light beige brown floss, sew sawtooth hanger to center top backside of stitched piece. #

## COLOR KEY

| Worsted Weight Yarn | Yards |
|---|---|
| ■ Dark blue green | 4 |
| ▨ Medium blue green | 3 |
| ▨ Light blue green | 3 |
| ▨ Medium terra cotta | 3 |
| ▢ Light gray | 3 |
| ▢ Light terra cotta | 2 |
| ■ Bronze | 2 |
| ▨ Medium brown | 2 |
| ■ Black | 1 |
| ▨ Yellow gold | 1 |
| ▢ Very light gold | 1 |
| ▨ Tan | 1 |
| ▢ Light sand | 1 |
| ■ Dark brown | 1 |
| ■ Medium charcoal | 1 |
| ╱ Black Straight Stitch | |

| Rayon Chenille Yarn | Yards |
|---|---|
| ▢ Ecru #2 | 11 |
| ▨ Ivory #3 | 16 |
| ▨ Beige #4 | 11 |
| ▨ Honey #7 | 19 |
| ▨ Lichen #26 | 10 |

Uncoded areas on kitten are
ecru #2 Continental Stitches

╱ Ecru #2 Straight Stitch

**#3 Pearl Cotton**
╱ Black Backstitch and
   Straight Stitch       5

**#5 Pearl Cotton**
╱ Black Backstitch and
   Straight Stitch       2

Color numbers given are for Honeysuckle
rayon chenille yarn by Elmore-Pisgah Inc.

**Kitty**
56 holes x 59 holes
Cut 1

**92** - - - - - *Plastic Canvas Stitch by Stitch*

**COLOR KEY**

| Plastic Canvas Yarn | Yards |
|---|---|
| ■ Fern #23 | 9 |
| ■ Moss #25 | 8 |
| □ White #41 | 4 |
| ■ Orchid #44 | 4 |

Color numbers given are for Uniek
Needloft plastic canvas yarn.

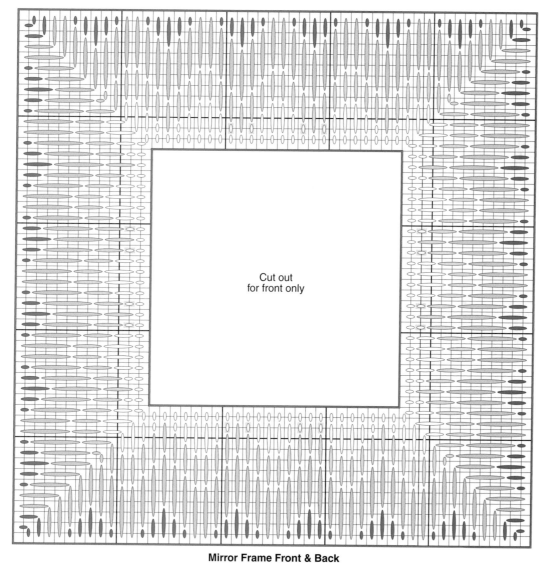

Cut out
for front only

**Mirror Frame Front & Back**
50 holes x 50 holes
Cut 2
Stitch front only

# Summer Shades Eyeglasses Case

Design by Judy Collishaw

This friendly little girl seems to only have eyes for you! With her country charm and 20-20 vision, she'll guard your eyeglasses in sugar-sweet style!

## Skill Level • Beginner

## Finished Size

4¼ inches W x 7⅛ inches H

## Materials

- 1 sheet 7-count plastic canvas
- Worsted weight yarn as listed in color key
- #5 pearl cotton as listed in color key
- #16 tapestry needle
- 2 (3/8-inch) buttons
- Hand-sewing needle
- Sewing thread to match buttons
- Hot-glue gun

## Instructions

**1** Cut plastic canvas according to graphs.

**2** Overcast one flower with royal blue as graphed, one with lavender and one with deep yellow. Work French Knots in center of flowers as follows: yellow in royal blue, deep yellow in lavender and brown in deep yellow.

**3** Stitch and Overcast eyeglasses and hands. Stitch remaining pieces following graphs, working uncoded areas with medium orchid Continental Stitches.

**4** When background stitching is completed, Backstitch mouth with 2 plies medium orchid. Work Straight Stitch between shoes with full ply medium orchid. Work Backstitches on apron with full strand white. Add Straight Stitches to patches with black pearl cotton.

**5** For each braid, cut three 6-inch lengths of yellow yarn. Braid for 1½ inches; tie off with medium blue yarn, making a bow. Stitch braids to front where indicated on graph.

**6** Using hand-sewing needle and thread, sew one button each to front and back where indicated on graphs.

**7** Using photo as a guide, glue sunglasses over face, covering braid attachments; glue ends of braid to front. Glue hands in place over flower stems at ends of sleeves; glue flower to tops of stems.

**8** Using medium orchid, Overcast top edges of front and back, then Whipstitch wrong sides of front and back together. #

**Flower**
3 holes x 3 holes
Cut 3
Stitch 1 as graphed
Stitch 1, replacing royal blue with lavender and yellow with deep yellow
Stitch 1, replacing royal blue with deep yellow and yellow with brown

## COLOR KEY

| Worsted Weight Yarn | Yards |
|---|---|
| ■ Medium blue | 8 |
| ☐ White | 4 |
| ■ Black | 4 |
| ☐ Peach | 3 |
| ☐ Yellow | 2 |
| ■ Rose | 1 |
| ☐ Light blue | 1 |
| ■ Kelly green | 1 |
| Uncoded areas are medium orchid Continental Stitches | 16 |
| ✎ Medium orchid Backstitch, Straight Stitch, Overcasting and Whipstitching | |
| ✎ Royal blue Overcasting | 1 |
| Lavender Overcasting | 1 |
| Deep yellow Overcasting | 1 |
| ✎ White Backstitch | |
| ○ Yellow French Knot | |
| Brown French Knot | 1 |
| **#5 Pearl Cotton** | |
| ✎ Black Straight Stitch | 1 |
| ● Attach button | |
| ● Attach braid | |

**Hands**
5 holes x 3 holes
Cut 1

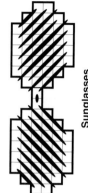

**Sunglasses**
18 holes x 6 holes
Cut 1

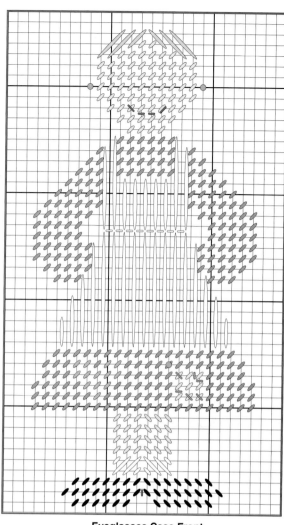

**Eyeglasses Case Front**
27 holes x 47 holes
Cut 1

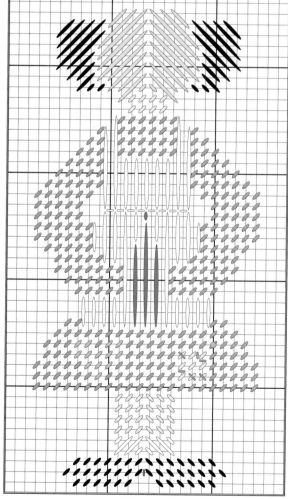

**Eyeglasses Case Back**
27 holes x 47 holes
Cut 1

Noah

found grace in the eyes
of the LORD.

Genesis 6:8

# CHAPTER FIVE

# Cross Stitch

## Cross Stitches add depth to your plastic canvas projects!

Take your plastic canvas projects proudly into the next dimension with the lovely addition of Cross Stitch patterns! In this

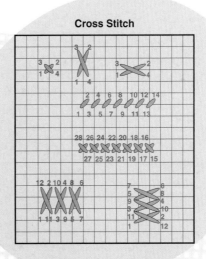

**Cross Stitch**

chapter you'll find a delightful variety of practical projects that illustrate the dimensional beauty and texture of these well-loved stitches!

# Noah's Sampler

*Design by Janelle Giese*

This exquisite sampler celebrates **hope and redemption** through the beloved story of Noah, from 40 days and nights spent tossing at sea to the peaceful promise of the rising rainbow.

## Skill Level • Advanced

## Finished Size

11⅛ inches W x 13¾ inches H

## Materials

- 2 artist-size sheets stiff 7-count plastic canvas
- Coats & Clark Red Heart Classic worsted weight yarn Art. E267 as listed in color key
- Kreinik Medium (#16) Braid as listed in color key
- #3 pearl cotton as listed in color key
- DMC #5 pearl cotton as listed in color key
- 6-strand embroidery floss: small amount light beige brown and colors to match buttons
- #16 tapestry needle
- Mill Hill Products hand-painted ceramic buttons from Gay Bowles Sales Inc.:
  Noah' Ark set #86072
  2 giraffes #86141
  2 lions #86144
- Sawtooth hanger

## Project Notes

Because colors on graph are close in color, please follow explanation of colors in instructions if help is needed in reading them.

## Preparation

**1** Join top and bottom graphs before cutting, then cut two 73-hole x 90-hole pieces according to graphs (pages 100 and 101).

**2** Place both 73-hole x 90-hole pieces together and work all stitches through both layers, following instructions below.

## Borders & Water

**1** Continental Stitch moon and sun in corner motifs with eggshell and cornmeal, working uncoded background (shaded in blue) with Windsor blue Continental Stitches. Cross Stitch border around corner motifs with coffee and claret.

**2** Work remaining blue-shaded, uncoded borders with Windsor blue Continental Stitches.

**3** Work Smyrna Cross Stitches for second border design on vertical and horizontal rows. For first stitch nearest corner design: Cross Stitch, black; Upright Cross Stitch, coffee. Second and third stitches on vertical rows and second on horizontal rows: Cross Stitch, coffee; Upright Cross Stitch, mid brown.

**4** Work next three stitches on vertical rows and next two stitches on horizontal row: Cross Stitch, mid brown; Upright Cross Stitch, warm brown. All remaining Smyrna Cross Stitches: Cross Stitch, warm brown; Upright Cross Stitch, tan.

**5** Work a row of claret Cross Stitches on each side of pink-shaded uncoded areas, working black and coffee Cross Stitches as shown near corner motifs.

**6** Adjusting stitches to fit at end of each trip, stitch pink-shaded areas with a Six-Trip Herringbone Stitch, working in direction of arrows and using colors as follows: first trip, black; second, teal; third, Windsor blue; fourth, seafoam; fifth, light sage; sixth, light seafoam.

**7** Work Rice Stitches for remaining border design. For first stitch nearest corner design on vertical and horizontal rows: Cross Stitch, coffee; corner stitches, black. Second stitches from corner design on vertical and horizontal rows: Cross Stitch, mid brown; corner stitches, coffee.

**8** For third stitch from corner design on vertical rows: Cross Stitch, warm brown; corner stitches, mid brown. All remaining Rice Stitches: Cross Stitch, honey gold; corner stitches, medium coral. ***Note:*** *Work half of each Rice Stitch where indicated along sides at very bottom of rainbow.*

**9** Work bottom of piece with eggshell, white, seafoam, light seafoam, mist green and teal.

## Center Motif

**1** Beginning with Cross Stitches and the outside row, work main rainbow in alternating rows of Cross Stitches and Continental Stitches using colors in the following order: cameo rose, pink, medium coral, sea coral, cornmeal, maize, light sage, mist green, country blue, pale blue, light plum, light lavender.

**2** Using a double strand through step 3, work two Upright Cross Stitches below Cross Stitches in main rainbow, using cameo rose, medium coral, cornmeal, light sage, country blue and light plum. Below these, work upright Cross Stitches in shades used for Continental Stitches of rainbow.

**3** Work remaining Upright Cross Stitches below rainbow with pale blue. Work eggshell and tan Cross Stitches where indicated.

**4** Work lettering with claret, coffee and black Continental Stitches and Cross Stitches.

**5** Stitch Noah's mountain with tan, warm brown, medium brown and light sage. Stitch remaining center area with warm brown and tan Continental Stitches, eggshell Cross Stitches and eggshell Continental Stitches in uncoded area.

## Overcasting & Embroidery

**1** Overcast water edges with seafoam, teal and eggshell. Overcast remaining edges with black.

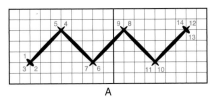

A
Work first trip with first color, bringing needle up on 1, down on 2, up on 3, down on 4, etc.

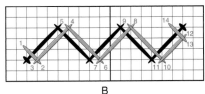

B
Work second trip with second color, bringing needle up on 1, down on 2, etc.

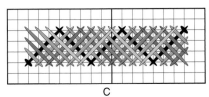

C
Continue working each trip with a different color until all six trips are completed.

**Six-Trip Herringbone Stitch**

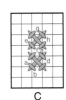

A
Work stitches on graph A first, coming up at 1, going down at 2, up at 3, down at 4, etc.

B
Work stitches on graph B next, coming up at A, going down at B, up at C, down at D, etc.

C
Work stitches on graph C last, coming up at a, going down at b, up at c, down at d, etc.

**Rice Stitch**

| COLOR KEY | |
|---|---|
| **Worsted Weight Yarn** | **Yards** |
| ☐ White #1 | 1 |
| ■ Black #12 | 9 |
| ▨ Teal #48 | 6 |
| ☐ Eggshell #111 | 38 |
| ☐ Cornmeal #220 | 4 |
| ☐ Sea coral #246 | 2 |
| ▨ Medium coral #252 | 6 |
| ☐ Maize #261 | 2 |
| ☐ Tan #334 | 8 |
| ▨ Warm brown #336 | 8 |
| ▨ Mid brown #339 | 4 |
| ■ Coffee #365 | 5 |
| ▨ Light plum #531 | 3 |
| ☐ Light lavender #579 | 2 |
| ☐ Light sage #631 | 5 |
| ☐ Honey gold #645 | 3 |
| ☐ Mist green #681 | 5 |
| ☐ Light seafoam #683 | 6 |
| ▨ Seafoam #684 | 9 |
| ☐ Pink #737 | 2 |
| ▨ Cameo rose #759 | 3 |
| ■ Claret #762 | 10 |
| ▨ Windsor blue #808 | 10 |
| ☐ Pale blue #815 | 7 |
| ▨ Country blue #882 | 3 |
| Uncoded area below rainbow is eggshell #111 Continental Stitches | |
| Uncoded areas in shaded blue areas are Windsor blue #808 Continental Stitches | |
| ⁄ Claret #762 Straight Stitch | |
| **Medium (#16) Braid** | |
| ⁄ Pearl #032 Straight Stitch and Cross Stitch | 9 |
| ⁄ Vatican gold #102 Backstitch, Straight Stitch and Smyrna Cross Stitch | 7 |
| **#3 Pearl Cotton** | |
| ⁄ Black Backstitch | 4 |
| **#5 Pearl Cotton** | |
| ⁄ Black brown #3371 Backstitch and Straight Stitch | 8 |
| ● Black brown #3371 French Knot | |
| Color numbers given are for Coats & Clark Red Heart Classic worsted weight yarn Art. E267, Kreinik Medium (#16) Braid and DMC #5 pearl cotton. | |

**2** Using pearl medium braid, work Straight Stitches over mist green Continental Stitches in water and on Continental Stitches in rainbow. Work Cross Stitches over pink, sea coral, maize, mist green, pale blue and light lavender Upright Cross Stitches at very bottom of rainbow.

**3** Using Vatican gold medium braid throughout, work Smyrna Cross Stitches on the letter "N." Work Backstitches and Straight Stitches on water, letters, rainbow and corner sun and moon motifs.

**4** Straight Stitch center bar on the letter "N" with claret. Use black #3 pearl cotton to Straight Stitch below claret Straight Stitch.

**5** Using black brown #5 and black #3 pearl cotton, work remaining embroidery.

## Finishing

**1** Using photo as a guide, attach buttons to finished piece with matching floss.

**2** Using light beige brown floss, sew sawtooth hanger to center top backside of finished piece behind Smyrna Cross Stitches. #

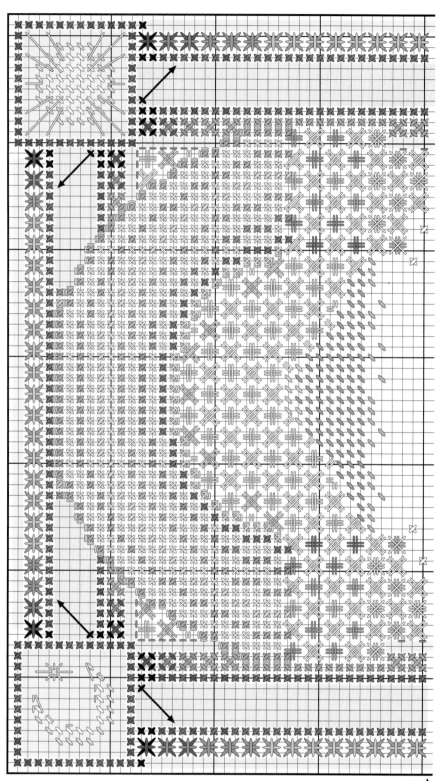

**Noah's Sampler (Top Part)**
73 holes x 90 holes

Joining Row
Do not repeat
this row →

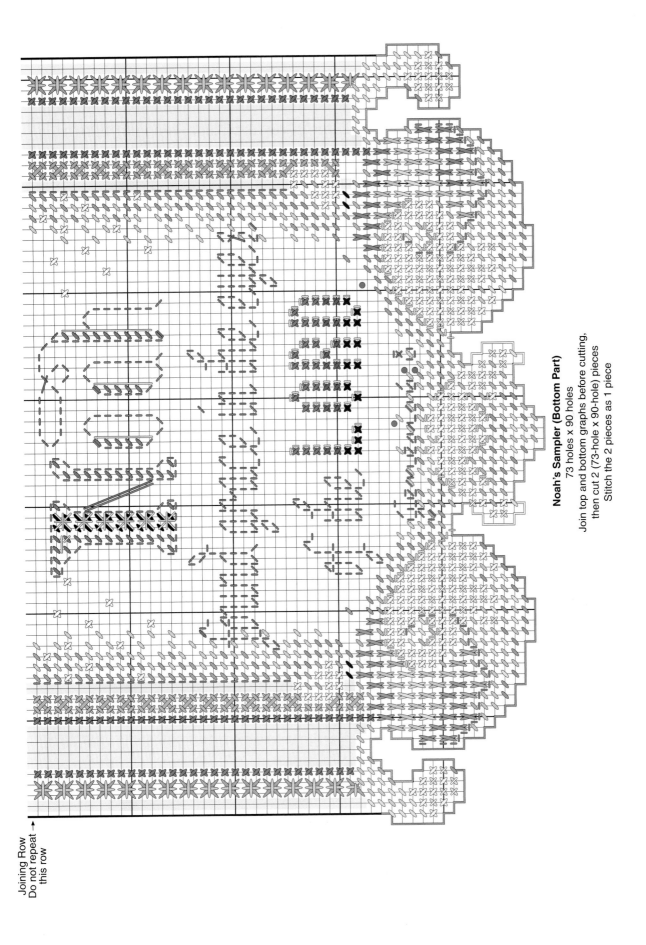

**Noah's Sampler (Bottom Part)**
73 holes x 90 holes
Join top and bottom graphs before cutting,
then cut 2 (73-hole x 90-hole) pieces
Stitch the 2 pieces as 1 piece

Joining Row →
Do not repeat
this row

# Shadow Lace & Roses

Design by Judy Collishaw

Delicate roses nestle in a plush garden of **textured lace**, blooming when needed to sweeten the air and soothe your soul!

## Skill Level • Intermediate

## Finished Size
Fits boutique-style tissue box

## Materials

- 1½ sheets 7-count plastic canvas
- Worsted weight yarn as listed in color key
- #5 pearl cotton as listed in color key
- #16 tapestry needle

## Instructions

**1** Cut plastic canvas according to graphs.

**2** Work dusty rose Upright Cross Stitches first, then work white Cross Stitches over dusty rose stitches. Work uncoded areas on sides with white Continental Stitches; work uncoded areas on top with Reverse Continental Stitches.

**3** When background stitching is completed, work Rose Stitches following Fig. 1.

**4** Using dusty rose throughout, Overcast inside edges of top and bottom edges of sides. Whipstitch sides together, then Whipstitch sides to top. #

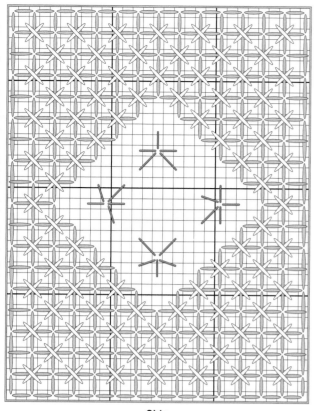

**Side**
29 holes x 37 holes
Cut 4

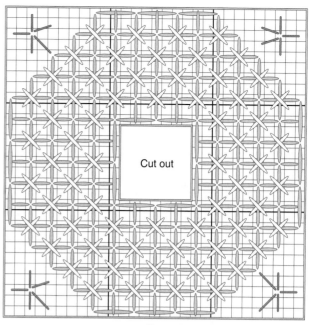

**Top**
29 holes x 29 holes
Cut 1

| COLOR KEY | |
|---|---|
| **Worsted Weight Yarn** | **Yards** |
| ☐ Dusty rose | 42 |
| ☐ White | 35 |
| Uncoded areas on sides are white Continental Stitches | |
| Uncoded areas on top are white Reverse Continental Stitches | |
| ✎ Wine Rose Stitch | 7 |
| **#5 Pearl Cotton** | |
| ✎ Kelly green Straight Stitch | 5 |

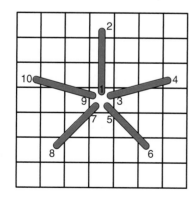

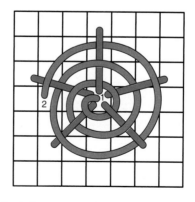

First, Straight Stitch five kelly green pearl
cotton spokes from the same center hole.
Next, using wine yarn, bring needle up through
center hole and begin weaving over and under spokes,
keeping tension slightly loose. Continue weaving
from center out until rose is an even ¹/₂-inch in diameter.
Draw yarn slightly to puff up rose and cover inner green stitches,
leaving a little kelly green showing at edges of roses for leaves.
Bring needle to backside and fasten off.

**Fig. 1**
**Rose Stitch**

# Gingham Scallops Coasters

Designs by Kimberly A. Suber

Serve your guests with a **rainbow of cheer** by setting your table with a quintet of colorful coasters!

## Finished Size

4½ inches square

## Materials

**One coaster**

- ¼ sheet 7-count plastic canvas
- Worsted weight yarn as listed in color key (see Project Note)
- #16 tapestry needle

## Project Note

Samples were completed in shades of blue, green, purple, yellow and rose. Three shades in each color range were used.

Instructions and yardage given are for one coaster.

## Instructions

**1** Cut plastic canvas according to graph.

**2** Stitch coaster following graph, working the Upright Cross Stitch first, then the Cross Stitch on top. Overcast with medium shade. #

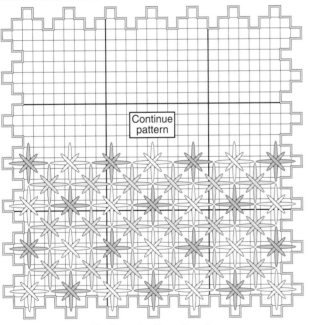

**Gingham Scallops Coaster**
29 holes x 29 holes
Cut 1

| COLOR KEY | |
|---|---|
| **Worsted Weight Yarn** | **Yards** |
| ☐ Medium shade | 7 |
| ▨ Dark shade | 4 |
| ☐ Light shade | 4 |

Continue pattern

# Pretty Posies Eyeglasses Case

Design by Maryanne Moreck

As **fresh and delightful** as a meadow in springtime, this beautiful handful of posies will mind your glasses in flowery style!

## Skill Level • Beginner

## Finished Size

4⅛ inches W x 7 inches H

## Materials

- ½ sheet 7-count plastic canvas
- Worsted weight yarn as listed in color key
- #16 tapestry needle

## Instructions

**1** Cut plastic canvas according to graph.

**2** Stitch pieces following graphs, working uncoded areas with white Continental Stitches. For Smyrna Cross Stitches, work Upright Cross Stitches first, then work Cross Stitches on top.

**3** Using white, Overcast top edges; Whipstitch wrong sides of pieces together around side and bottom edges. #

| COLOR KEY | |
|---|---|
| **Worsted Weight Yarn** | **Yards** |
| ☐ White | 20 |
| ▩ Dark green | 8 |
| ▨ Dark rose | 2 |
| ☐ Light rose | 2 |
| ☐ Light green | 1 |
| ■ Black | 1 |
| Uncoded areas are white Continental Stitches | |

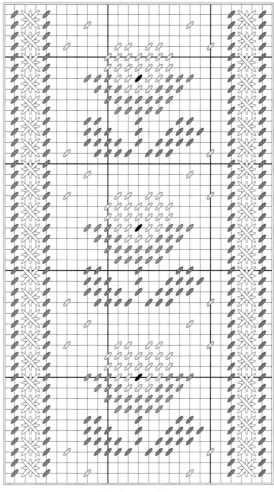

**Eyeglasses Case**
26 holes x 45 holes
Cut 2

# Potpourri Box

Design by Kathy Wirth

Open, airy stitches and **cutouts in the lid** make this
elegant box perfect for holding your favorite fragrance of potpourri!

## Skill Level • Intermediate

## Finished Size

6½ inches diameter x 4¾ inches H,
including pearl bead knob

## Materials

- 2 sheets clear 7-count plastic canvas
- ⅔ sheet white 7-count plastic canvas
- 6-inch plastic canvas radial circle by Darice
- Coats & Clark Red Heart Classic

worsted weight yarn Art. E267 as listed in color key

- ⅛-inch-wide Plastic Canvas 7 Metallic Needlepoint Yarn from Rainbow Gallery as listed in color key
- #16 tapestry needle
- #22 tapestry needle
- 16mm pearl bead
- White self-adhesive Presto felt from Kunin Felt
- Potpourri
- White glue

## Project Notes

When stitching with metallic needlepoint yarn, keep yarn smooth and flat.

Use #16 tapestry needle with worsted weight yarn. Use #22 needle with metallic needlepoint yarn.

## Instructions

**1** Cut two sides and one lid from

clear plastic canvas; cut one lid and two lid lips from white plastic canvas according to graphs (page 109).

**2** For box bottom, cut one row off outer edge of plastic canvas radial circle. Bottom will remain unstitched. From white felt, cut a circle slightly smaller all around than bottom.

**3** Stitch sides and clear lid following graphs, overlapping three holes

of side pieces together before stitching, forming a circle 5⅞-inches in diameter. Do not stitch white lid liner.

**4** Whipstitch bottom edge of sides to unstitched bottom with light berry. Overcast top edge with off-white.

**5** Overlap lid lips as indicated and stitch together where shown, forming a 5⅜-inch circle. Using off-white, Whipstitch to white lid

liner in location of green highlighted circle, leaving enough room to Whipstitch inside edges.

**6** Whipstitch wrong sides of clear and white lid pieces together, along inside edges with light berry and around outside edge with gold.

**7** Adhere white felt circle to bottom inside box. Glue pearl bead to center top of stitched lid. #

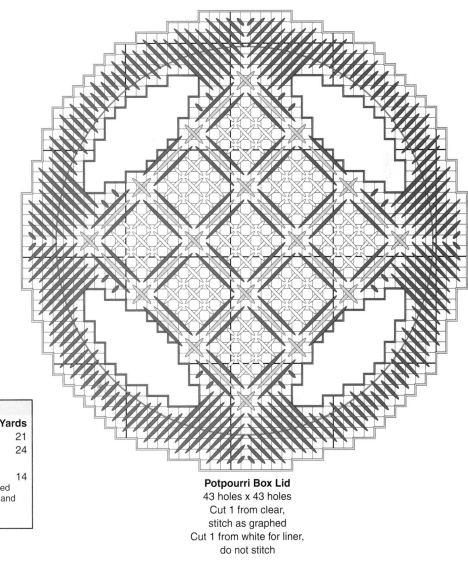

Potpourri Box Lid
43 holes x 43 holes
Cut 1 from clear,
stitch as graphed
Cut 1 from white for liner,
do not stitch

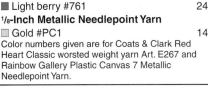

**COLOR KEY**

| Worsted Weight Yarn | Yards |
|---|---|
| ☐ Off-white #3 | 21 |
| ■ Light berry #761 | 24 |

**⅛-Inch Metallic Needlepoint Yarn**

| | |
|---|---|
| ☐ Gold #PC1 | 14 |

Color numbers given are for Coats & Clark Red Heart Classic worsted weight yarn Art. E267 and Rainbow Gallery Plastic Canvas 7 Metallic Needlepoint Yarn.

Potpourri Box Lid Lip
58 holes x 4 holes
Cut 2 from white

# Delicate Sachet Set

Designs by Maryanne Moreck

Soft pastel colors and **delicate stitches** make these beautiful sachets a fragrant delight!

## Skill Level • Beginner

## Finished Size

4⅛ inches square

## Materials

- ½ sheet 7-count plastic canvas
- Worsted weight yarn as listed in color key
- #16 tapestry needle
- 24 inches ¼-inch-wide ivory satin ribbon
- 2 (3-inch x 3-inch) squares batting
- Scented oil or powder

## Instructions

**1** Cut plastic canvas according to graphs. Back pieces will remain unstitched.

**2** Stitch front pieces following graphs. For Smyrna Cross Stitches on pink sachet, work Upright Cross Stitches first, then work Cross Stitches on top.

**3** On light aqua sachet, work eggshell and light aqua Smyrna Cross Stitches following instructions in step 2. For two-color Smyrna Cross Stitches, work light aqua Cross Stitches first then work eggshell Upright Cross Stitches on top.

**4** Overcast inside edges on fronts and backs with eggshell. Lightly moisten or powder batting with desired scent and place between front and back. Whipstitch fronts and backs together with eggshell.

**5** Cut ribbon into four 6-inch lengths. For each sachet, thread one length through hole; tie in a knot on backside and glue in place. Tie each remaining length in a bow; glue to front pieces over holes.

**6** To re-scent batting, powder or lightly moisten with scented oil. #

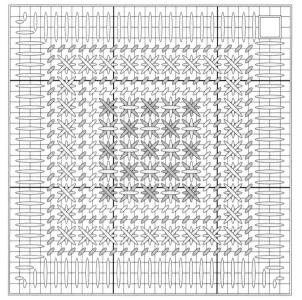

**Light Aqua Sachet**
27 holes x 27 holes
Cut 2, stitch 1

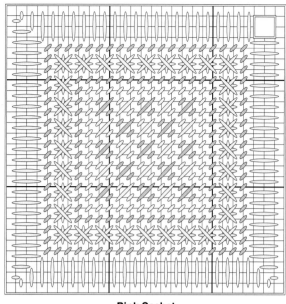

**Pink Sachet**
27 holes x 27 holes
Cut 2, stitch 1

| COLOR KEY | |
|---|---|
| **Worsted Weight Yarn** | **Yards** |
| ☐ Eggshell | 20 |
| ☐ Light aqua | 6 |
| ☐ Rose pink | 4 |

## Potpourri Box continued from page 107 —  —  —  —  —  —  —  —  —  —

| COLOR KEY | |
|---|---|
| **Worsted Weight Yarn** | **Yards** |
| ☐ Off-white #3 | 21 |
| ■ Light berry #761 | 24 |
| **⅛-Inch Metallic Needlepoint Yarn** | |
| ☐ Gold #PC1 | 14 |
| Color numbers given are for Coats & Clark Red Heart Classic worsted weight yarn Art. E267 and Rainbow Gallery Plastic Canvas 7 Metallic Needlepoint Yarn. | |

Overlap  Overlap

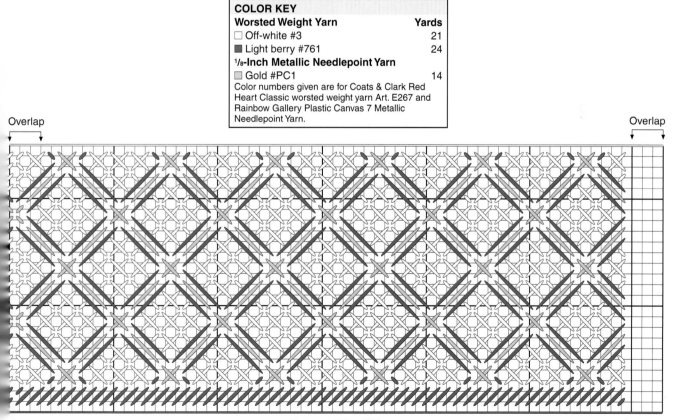

**Potpourri Box Side**
63 holes x 25 holes
Cut 2 from clear

# Golden Crocuses Boxes

Designs by Ruby Thacker

You'll see how practical a **pretty project** can be when you
stitch these golden-glowing floral boxes!

## Skill Level • Beginner

## Finished Size

**Large Box:** 4½ inches W x 5⅜
inches H

**Small Box:** 3⅝ inches W x 3¾
inches H

## Materials

- 2 sheets 7-count plastic canvas
- Uniek Needloft plastic canvas yarn as
  listed in color key
- 6-strand metallic embroidery floss as
  listed in color key
- #16 tapestry needle

- Large 4¾-inch-wide x 5⅜-inch-high
  plastic box with flat lid #75068
  from Plaid
- Medium 4-inch-wide x 4-inch-high
  plastic box with flat lid #75069
  from Plaid
- Clamps or weighted object
- Clear drying glue

## Instructions

**1** Cut plastic canvas according to
graphs. Cut one 29-hole x 29-hole
piece for large box bottom and
one 23-hole x 23-hole piece for
small box bottom. Bottom pieces
will remain unstitched.

**2** Stitch pieces following graphs,
working uncoded areas with
eggshell Continental Stitches.

**3** When background stitching
is completed, work fern and
Christmas green Straight Stitches
for leaves and black Straight
Stitches for butterfly antennae.
Using 3-plies gold metallic floss,
work Backstitches next to Smyrna
Cross Stitches.

**4** Using tangerine throughout,
Overcast lids and top edges of
sides. For large box, Whipstitch

sides together, then Whipstitch sides to large box bottom. Repeat for small box.

**5** Place stitched large box in large plastic box. Center stitched lid in plastic lid; using glue sparingly, attach right side of

stitched lid to plastic box lid; clamp or place weighted object on lid until dry.

**6** Repeat with remaining small box pieces and smaller plastic box. #

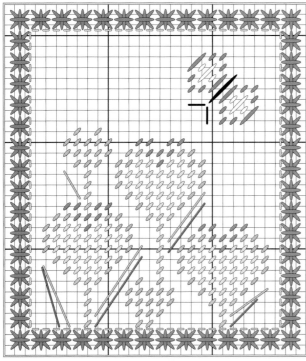

**Large Box Side**
29 holes x 33 holes
Cut 4

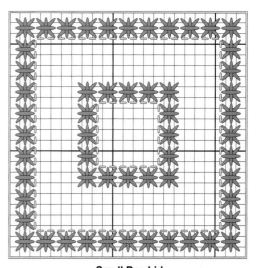

**Small Box Lid**
23 holes x 23 holes
Cut 1

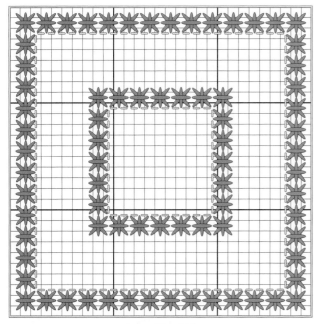

**Large Box Lid**
29 holes x 29 holes
Cut 1

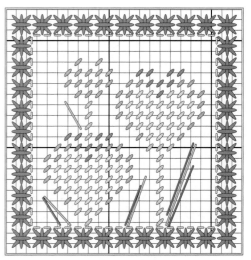

**Small Box Side**
23 holes x 23 holes
Cut 4

# Coaster Ensemble

Designs by Ruby Thacker

Reminiscent of **brilliant autumn leaves** and the delicious flavor of the harvest season, these radiant coasters make the perfect accent for fall decorating!

## Skill Level • Intermediate

## Finished Size

**Coasters:** 3⅞ inches square

**Holder:** 4⅜ inches square x 2 inches H

## Materials

- 1½ sheets 7-count plastic canvas
- Uniek Needloft plastic canvas yarn as listed in color key
- 6-strand metallic embroidery floss as listed in color key
- #16 tapestry needle

## Holder

**1** Cut holder pieces from plastic canvas according to graphs (pages 114 and 115).

**2** Stitch pieces following graphs, working uncoded areas with eggshell Continental Stitches.

**3** Using pumpkin, Whipstitch sides

to back and to outside side edges of front pieces.

**4** Using tangerine throughout, Overcast top edges of front, back and side pieces; Overcast inside edges of front pieces and front edge of bottom between arrows. Whipstitch front, back and side pieces to unstitched edges of bottom, keeping right side of bottom facing up.

## Coasters

**1** Cut six coasters from plastic canvas following graphs (this page and page 114).

**2** Stitch coasters B, D and F, working uncoded areas on coaster B with eggshell Continental Stitches and uncoded areas on coaster D with rust Continental Stitches.

**3** Overcast each with tangerine; work gold floss Backstitches.

**4** Stitch coaster A, working uncoded areas with eggshell Continental Stitches and Waffle Stitches with rust following diagram (page 115). Overcast with tangerine; work gold floss Backstitches.

**5** Stitch coaster C, working Tied Windmill Stitches with rust and pumpkin following diagram (page 115). Overcast with tangerine; work gold floss Backstitches.

**6** Stitch coaster E, working Diagonal Leaf Stitches with rust and Smooth Spiderweb Stitch with pumpkin following diagrams (page 115). Overcast with tangerine; work gold floss Backstitches. #

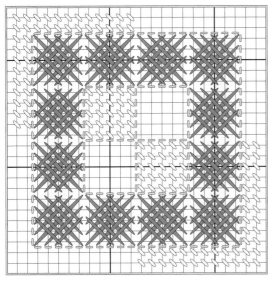

**Coaster A**
25 holes x 25 holes
Cut 1

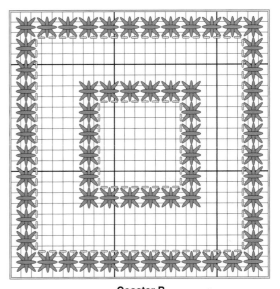

**Coaster B**
25 holes x 25 holes
Cut 1

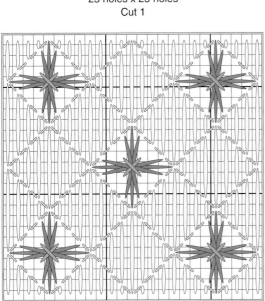

**Coaster C**
25 holes x 25 holes
Cut 1

| COLOR KEY | |
|---|---|
| **Plastic Canvas Yarn** | **Yards** |
| ■ Rust #09 | 22 |
| ☐ Tangerine #11 | 22 |
| ▨ Pumpkin #12 | 16 |
| ☐ Eggshell #39 | 37 |
| Uncoded areas on coaster D are rust #09 Continental Stitches | |
| Uncoded areas on holder pieces and coasters A and B are eggshell #39 Continental Stitches | |
| ⁄ Pumpkin #12 Straight Stitch | |
| **6-Strand Metallic Embroidery Floss** | |
| ⁄ Gold Backstitch | 8 |
| Color numbers given are for Uniek Needloft plastic canvas yarn. | |

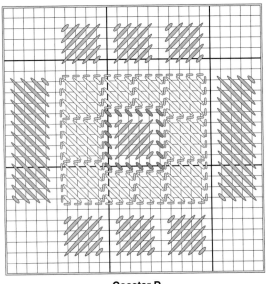

**Coaster D**
25 holes x 25 holes
Cut 1

**Coaster E**
25 holes x 25 holes
Cut 1

Back Edge

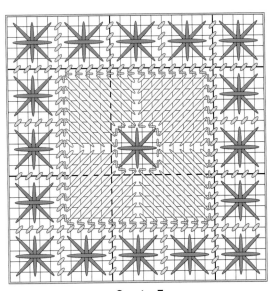

**Coaster F**
25 holes x 25 holes
Cut 1

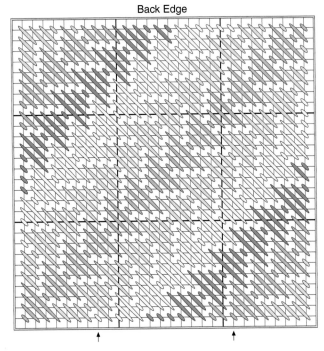

**Holder Bottom**
29 holes x 29 holes
Cut 1

**COLOR KEY**

| Plastic Canvas Yarn | Yards |
|---|---|
| ■ Rust #09 | 22 |
| □ Tangerine #11 | 22 |
| ■ Pumpkin #12 | 16 |
| □ Eggshell #39 | 37 |

Uncoded areas on coaster D are
rust #09 Continental Stitches
Uncoded areas on holder pieces and coasters
A and B are eggshell #39 Continental Stitches
⟋ Pumpkin #12 Straight Stitch
**6-Strand Metallic Embroidery Floss**

| | |
|---|---|
| ⟋ Gold Backstitch | 8 |

Color numbers given are for Uniek Needloft plastic canvas yarn.

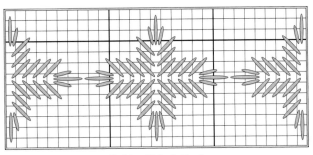

**Holder Side & Back**
29 holes x 13 holes
Cut 3

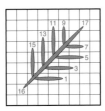

**Diagonal Leaf Stitch**
Using rust yarn, work stitches in order
given, adding Slanted Gobelin Stitch last

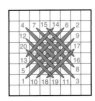

**Waffle Stitch**
Using rust yarn, bring needle
up at 1, down at 2,
up at 3, down at 4, etc.,
making sure to work stitches
in order given for the waffle look

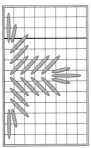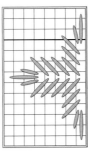

**Holder Front**
8 holes x 13 holes each
Cut 1 set

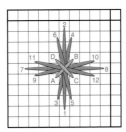

**Tied Windmill Stitch**
Using rust yarn, bring needle up at 1,
down at 2, up at 3, down at 4, etc.
When numbered stitches are completed,
work lettered stitches with pumpkin yarn,
bringing needle up at A, down at B,
up at C, down at D

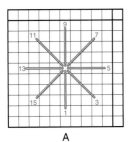

**A**
Using pumpkin yarn,
work spokes as indicated.

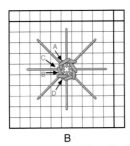

**B**
Using a 1½ yard length of
pumpkin yarn, weave yarn around
spokes, coming up at A, over two
spokes and down at B.
Go back under one spoke and come
up at C, over two and down at D.
Continue pattern, working first trip
completely around spokes.

**Smooth Spiderweb Stitch**

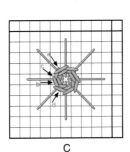

**C**
For second and subsequent
trips, continue weaving up
over two, back under one,
up over two, etc., until each trip
is completed and spokes are full.
Bring last stitch down
and secure on backside.

# Aquamarine & Pearls Photo Frame

Design by Kimberly A. Suber

Treat your favorite photos like the treasures they are with the **pearl-adorned lattice** and sparkling metallics of this eye-catching frame!

## Skill Level • Beginner

## Finished Size

7½ inches W x 6¼ inches H;
opening is 4½ inches x 3⅜ inches

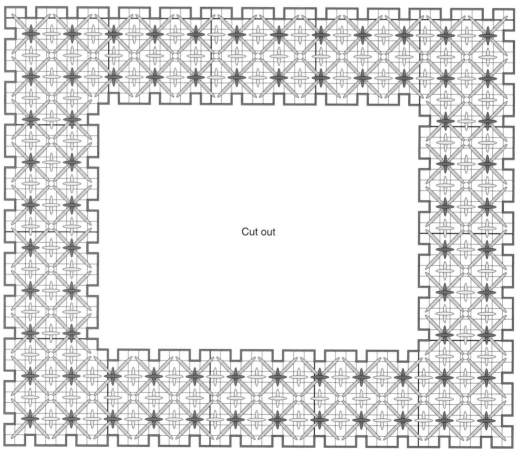

**Frame Front**
49 holes x 41 holes
Cut 1

## Materials

- 1 sheet 7-count plastic canvas
- Metallic cord as listed in color key
- Small amount aqua yarn
- #16 tapestry needle
- 36 (4mm) white pearl beads
- Hand-sewing needle
- White sewing thread

## Instructions

**1** Cut plastic canvas according to graph, cutting out holes on front and back. Cut one 19-hole x 28-hole piece for frame stand. Frame back and stand will remain unstitched.

**2** Stitch front following graph; Overcast inside edges with teal.

**3** Using hand-sewing needle and white thread, attach beads to front where indicated on graph.

**4** Using aqua yarn, Whipstitch stand to frame back where indicated on graph with blue highlighted line.

**5** Whipstitch frame front and back together with teal metallic cord. #

| COLOR KEY | |
|---|---|
| **Metallic Cord** | **Yards** |
| ■ Teal | 13 |
| ▨ Aqua/silver | 13 |
| ☐ Turquoise | 11 |
| ○ Attach white pearl bead | |

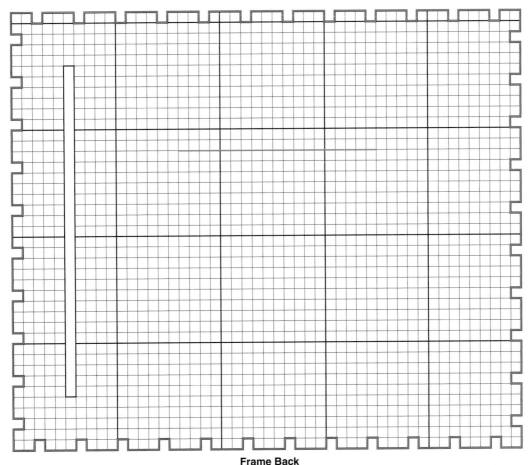

**Frame Back**
49 holes x 41 holes
Cut 1
Do not stitch

# CHAPTER SIX

# Square Stitch

**Square stitches are a quick way to fill backgrounds.**

Celebrate the neat and orderly potential of simple square stitches!

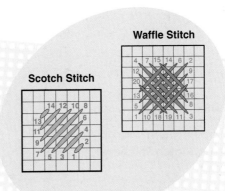

Scotch Stitch

Waffle Stitch

In this diverse and exciting collection, we offer a treasure trove of fabulous projects to expand your creativity and beautify your home!

# Tropical Toucan

*Design by Ronda Bryce*

With its **simple stitches and vibrant hues,** this sun-drenched toucan brings tropical warmth to your home in a flash!

## Skill Level • Beginner

## Finished Size

$7\frac{9}{16}$ inches W x $9\frac{7}{16}$ inches H, excluding frame

## Materials

- 1 sheet 7-count plastic canvas
- Uniek Needloft plastic canvas yarn as listed in color key
- #16 tapestry needle
- 11-inch x 14-inch black mat with 7½-inch x 9½-inch opening
- 12½-inch 15¾-inch frame with 10½-inch x 13½-inch opening
- Masking tape

## Instructions

**1** Cut plastic canvas according to graph.

**2** Stitch piece following graph, working uncoded areas with bright blue Scotch Stitches over three bars. Do not Overcast.

**3** Work black French Knot for eye and yellow French Knots for flower centers when background stitching is completed.

**4** Center and tape stitched piece behind opening on mat. Secure mat in frame. Hang as desired. #

| COLOR KEY | |
|---|---|
| **Plastic Canvas Yarn** | **Yards** |
| ■ Black #00 | 9 |
| ■ Red #01 | 3 |
| □ Christmas red #02 | 2 |
| ■ Burgundy #03 | 2 |
| ■ Cinnamon #14 | 5 |
| □ Gold #17 | 3 |
| □ Lemon #20 | 2 |
| ■ Fern #23 | 3 |
| ■ Christmas green #28 | 3 |
| □ Silver #37 | 18 |
| □ Camel #43 | 3 |
| ■ Turquoise #54 | 5 |
| □ Yellow #57 | 3 |
| □ Bright blue #60 | 14 |
| Uncoded areas are bright blue #60 Scotch Stitches | |
| ● Black #00 French Knot | |
| ○ Yellow #57 French Knot | |
| Color numbers given are for Uniek Needloft plastic canvas yarn. | |

**Tropical Toucan**
53 holes x 66 holes
Cut 1

# Create-Your-Own Patchwork

Designs by Alida Macor

With the mix-and-match patterns of this quilt-inspired set,
you can create your own showcase of quaint country charm!

## Skill Level • Beginner

## Finished Size

**Coaster:** 3½ inches square

**Table Runner:** 28¼ inches W x 10⅝ inches L, excluding fringe

**Place Mat (not shown):** 14⅛ inches W x 10⅝ inches L, excluding fringe

**Table Scarf:** Approximately 7 inches square, excluding fringe

## Materials

- 2 sheets soft 7-count plastic canvas
- Uniek Needloft plastic canvas yarn as listed in color key
- 32 yards (1 skein) DMC #3 pearl cotton as listed in color key
- 108 yards (4 skeins) DMC #5 pearl cotton as listed in color key
- #16 tapestry needle
- Off-white felt (optional)
- Craft glue

## Project Notes

Read instructions carefully to know when to use #3 and #5 pearl cotton.

Work squares in colors given or as desired (see samples in photo).

For coasters, work a total of eight squares as desired or work two of each for a set of eight.

For table scarf, work a total of four squares, using one design, a combination of two designs or all four designs.

## Cutting & Stitching

**1** Cut plastic canvas according to graphs and project notes (page 124).

**2** Stitch pieces following graphs. Overcast edges of coasters with off-white #3 pearl cotton and back with felt if desired.

## Table Runner Assembly

**1** Using ¾ yard off-white #5 pearl cotton per side, Whipstitch squares together in rows of three (see diagram on page 124), working first in one direction, then returning in opposite direction.

**2** Using 2½ yards off-white #5 pearl cotton per row, Whipstitch eight rows of three together following instructions in step 1.

**3** For fringe, cut 276 (9-inch) lengths off-white #5 pearl cotton. Attach two lengths to each hole on short ends with a Lark's Head Knot.

**4** Overcast long sides with off-white #3 pearl cotton.

## Place Mat Assembly

**1** Whipstitch squares together following assembly diagram (page 124) and steps 1 and 2 of table runner assembly.

**2** Following steps 3 and 4 of table runner assembly, attach fringe to sides edges and Overcast long edges.

## Table Scarf Assembly

**1** Whipstitch four squares together with #5 pearl cotton, working first in one direction, then returning in opposite direction.

**2** Attach fringe to sides (184 lengths total) as in table runner assembly, trimming to 1½ inches.

**3** Overcast remaining edges with #3 pearl cotton. #

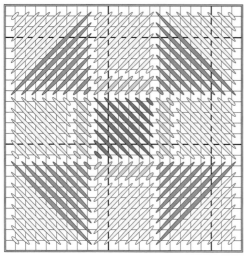

**Square A**
23 holes x 23 holes
Cut 6 for table runner
Cut 3 for place mat
Cut as desired for coaster
and table scarf

**Square B**
23 holes x 23 holes
Cut 6 for table runner
Cut 3 for place mat
Cut as desired for coaster
and table scarf

**Square C**
23 holes x 23 holes
Cut 6 for table runner
Cut 3 for place mat
Cut as desired for coaster
and table scarf

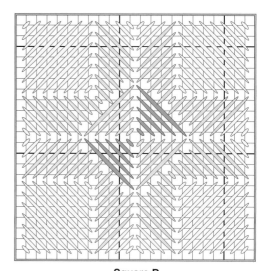

**Square D**
23 holes x 23 holes
Cut 6 for table runner
Cut 3 for place mat
Cut as desired for coaster
and table scarf

| COLOR KEY | |
|---|---|
| **Plastic Canvas Yarn** | **Yards** |
| ■ Lavender #05 | 14 |
| □ Moss #25 | 23 |
| □ Baby blue #36 | 21 |
| □ Eggshell #39 | 90 |
| □ Orchid #44 | 9 |
| ■ Lilac #45 | 18 |
| ■ Mermaid #53 | 8 |
| **#3 and #5 Pearl Cotton** | |
| ⁄ Off-white #746 Overcasting and Whipstitching | |

Color numbers given are for Uniek
Needloft plastic canvas yarn and DMC #3
and #5 pearl cotton.

| D | A | B |
|---|---|---|
| C | D | A |
| B | C | D |
| A | B | C |
| D | A | B |
| C | D | A |
| B | C | D |
| A | B | C |

**Table Runner Diagram**

| A | B | C | D |
|---|---|---|---|
| D | A | B | C |
| C | D | A | B |

**Place Mat Diagram**

# Ojos de Dios Wall Hanging

Design by Pam Bull

Southwestern patterning and desert-rose tones give this "Eyes of God" piece a timeless sense of soothing calm.

## Skill Level • Intermediate

### Finished Size
4¾ inches W x 15 inches L, excluding tassels and hanger

## Materials

- 1 sheet 10-count plastic canvas
- Soft worsted weight yarn as listed in color key
- #18 tapestry needle

## Instructions

**1** Combine left and right graphs (pages 126 and 127) before cutting, then cut one 106-hole x 106-hole piece from plastic canvas following graph, making sure not to repeat center bar and center area highlighted with blue.

**2** Stitch piece following graphs, working four Waffle Stitches (page 115) with dark yellow green. Overcast with camel.

**3** For hanger, thread one 16-inch length camel yarn through each hole indicated on graph; tie each in a knot, leaving a 2½-inch tail. Braid set of three on both sides, then knot each braid, leaving about a ½-inch tail. Tie braids together in a knot, leaving 3½-inch tails.

**4** For fringe, thread one end of a 12-inch length camel yarn through each hole indicated; knot securely in center. #

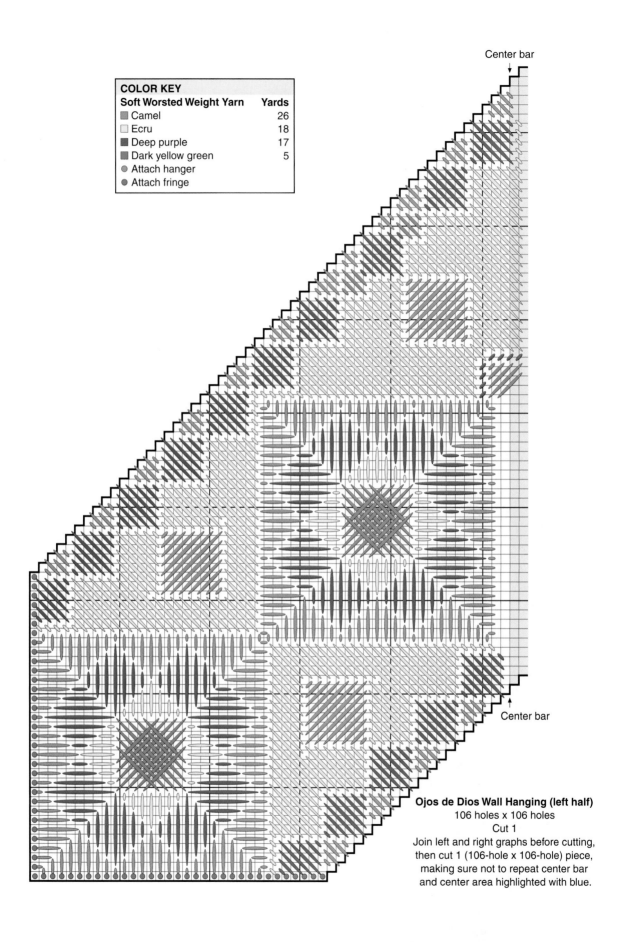

**COLOR KEY**

| Soft Worsted Weight Yarn | Yards |
|---|---|
| ■ Camel | 26 |
| □ Ecru | 18 |
| ■ Deep purple | 17 |
| ■ Dark yellow green | 5 |
| ● Attach hanger | |
| ● Attach fringe | |

Center bar

Center bar

**Ojos de Dios Wall Hanging (left half)**
106 holes x 106 holes
Cut 1
Join left and right graphs before cutting,
then cut 1 (106-hole x 106-hole) piece,
making sure not to repeat center bar
and center area highlighted with blue.

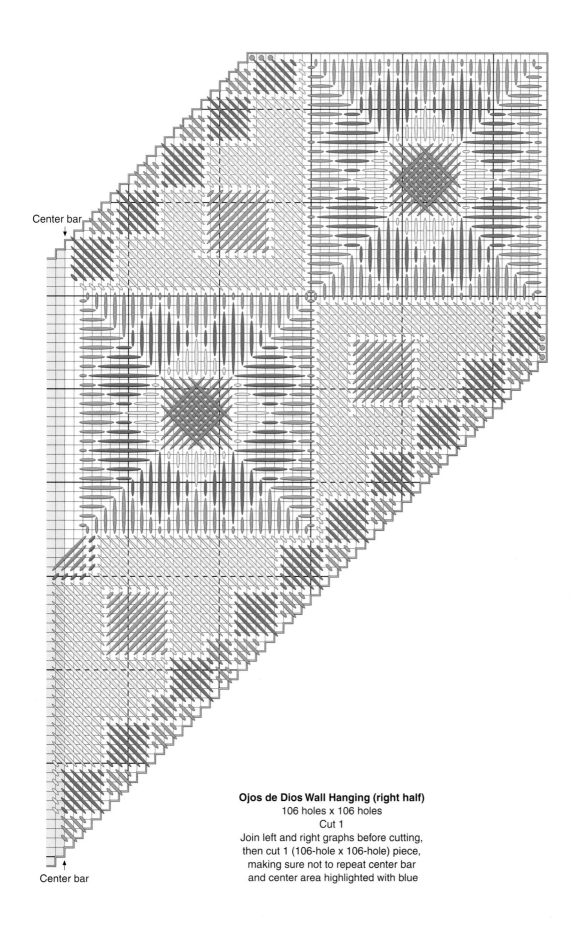

Center bar

Center bar

**Ojos de Dios Wall Hanging (right half)**
106 holes x 106 holes
Cut 1
Join left and right graphs before cutting,
then cut 1 (106-hole x 106-hole) piece,
making sure not to repeat center bar
and center area highlighted with blue

# Native American Patchwork Box

Design by Maryanne Moreck

Decorate your home in Southwestern style with the **sun-baked colors** and ancient patterning of this vibrant patchwork project!

## Skill Level • Beginner

## Finished Size

4¼ inches W x 2⅜ inches H x 4¼ inches D

## Materials

- 1 sheet 7-count plastic canvas
- Worsted weight yarn as listed in color key
- #16 tapestry needle

## Instructions

**1** Cut plastic canvas according to graphs (page 135).

**2** Stitch pieces following graphs, working uncoded border on lid with ivory Continental Stitches.

**3** Using ivory throughout, Overcast top edges of box sides and bottom edges of lid sides. Whipstitch box sides together, then with bottom piece facing up, Whipstitch sides to bottom. Whipstitch lid sides together, then Whipstitch sides to top. #

| COLOR KEY | |
|---|---|
| **Worsted Weight Yarn** | **Yards** |
| ☐ Ivory | 30 |
| ▨ Purple | 8 |
| ▨ Burgundy | 8 |
| ▨ Olive green | 4 |
| Uncoded border on lid is ivory Continental Stitches | |

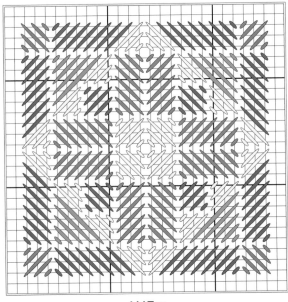

**Lid Top**
27 holes x 27 holes
Cut 1

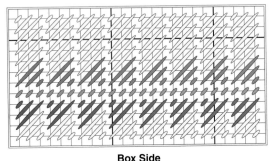

**Box Side**
25 holes x 13 holes
Cut 4

# Flowers on the Square & Good Luck Rainbow

Designs by Alida Macor

Shining with quiet beauty, these fine, **delicate bookmarks** create a peaceful calm to enhance your reading enjoyment!

## Skill Level • Beginner

### Finished Size

1³⁄₈ inches W x 5³⁄₈ inches H

## Materials

- ¼ sheet 10-count plastic canvas
- DMC 6-strand embroidery floss as listed in color key
- #18 tapestry needle
- 2 (1½-inch-long) white tassels

### Instructions

**1** Cut plastic canvas according to graphs (page 135).

**2** Stitch pieces following graphs. Overcast inside edges with white.

Using 1 yard white Overcast outer edges in every other hole.

**3** Attach tassels through hole at bottom of bookmarks with Lark's Head Knots. #

# Quilted Home

Design by Janelle Giese

Quaint, charming, **exquisitely detailed** and full of sweet sentiment,
this cheerful wall hanging will truly make your house a home!

## Skill Level • Advanced

## Finished Size

9¼ inches W x 16⅛ inches H

## Materials

- 1 sheet stiff 7-count plastic canvas
- ¼ sheet 10-count plastic canvas
- Coats & Clark Red Heart Classic worsted weight yarn Art. E267 as listed in color key
- DMC #3 pearl cotton as listed in color key
- DMC #5 pearl cotton as listed in color key
- #16 tapestry needle
- Small amounts 6-strand embroidery floss to match cameo rose and pale rose yarn
- 2 Mill Hill Products hand-painted ceramic tulip basket buttons #86036 from Gay Bowles Sales Inc.
- 1¼-inch-long gold eye pin
- 2 (7mm) gold jump rings
- Sawtooth hanger
- Thick white glue

## Project Notes

Because colors on graph are close in color, please follow explanation of colors in instructions if help is needed in reading them.

## Cutting

**1** Cut sign from 10-count plastic canvas according to graph (page 132).

**2** Cut house from 7-count stiff plastic canvas according to graph (page 133).

## Sign

**1** Using yarn through step 4, work each corner with light sage Reverse Mosaic Stitches (page 133), then work borders with Mosaic Stitches using pale rose, medium coral, honey gold, light sage, country blue and tan.

**2** Work one row of Continental Stitches around border and corners with dark sage.

**3** Work the letter "I" of the word "If" with Cross Stitches, using pale rose on top, then medium coral, honey gold, light sage and country blue.

**4** Work the word "QUILTS" with Cross Stitches, using pale rose on top, then medium coral and honey gold. Use light sage for bottom of tail in the letter "Q."

**5** Work background in center with pearl cotton Continental Stitches, using very light old gold near border; use cream in uncoded area.

**6** Overcast with black yarn. Embroider lettering and remaining details with very dark brown gray pearl cotton.

## Roof

**1** Using yarn through step 3, stitch coded areas at very top of roof with light sage and off-white Continental Stitches. Work uncoded areas with eggshell Continental Stitches.

**2** Stitch Windowpane Scotch Stitches (page 134), working the 15 center stitches with pale rose and light berry. Work the 13 partial Windowpane Scotch Stitches above and to the side of center stitches with cameo rose and new berry.

**3** Work bottom part of roof with dark sage and light sage Continental Stitches.

**4** Overcast roof area with light sage, off-white and dark sage yarn. Using #3 pearl cotton, work Backstitches with black and French Knots with cream.

## Windows, Door & Steps

**1** Using yarn through step 4, stitch uncoded areas of windows and doors with eggshell Continental Stitches. Stitch coded window and door areas with warm brown, tan and off-white.

**2** Work windowpanes with off-white and pale blue; work window shade with off-white. Stitch bottom panel in door with honey gold, cornmeal and medium coral, working four bronze stitches last.

**3** Work steps with bronze and medium coral, working French Knots with bronze.

**4** For door hardware, use a full strand honey gold to work two Straight Stitches, then work French Knot for knob, wrapping knot two times.

**5** Embroider details using very dark brown gray pearl cotton and cream pearl cotton. Beginning and ending in same hole, wrap very dark brown gray pearl cotton around honey gold French Knot. Do not work black pearl cotton embroidery at this time.

## Sunbonnet Sue & Ladder

**1** Using yarn through step 3, stitch and Overcast ladder with warm brown. Stitch and Overcast hand with tan. Stitch and Overcast dress and shoes with black and cornmeal.

**2** Stitch bonnet with bronze, medium coral and black, working leaf with dark sage. Overcast with bronze. Work dark sage Straight Stitch for second leaf.

**3** Work country blue French Knot for flower on hat, keeping tension loose and wrapping yarn around needle two times.

**4** Using pearl cotton through step 5, work French Knot for flower center, with very light old gold, coming up at center of yarn knot, wrapping pearl cotton around needle two times, then going down in the same hole.

## COLOR KEY

| Worsted Weight Yarn | Yards |
|---|---|
| ☐ Off-white #3 | 6 |
| ■ Black #12 | 5 |
| ☐ Cornmeal #220 | 3 |
| ▦ Medium coral #252 | 4 |
| ▦ Bronze #286 | 4 |
| ☐ Tan #334 | 5 |
| ■ Warm brown #336 | 5 |
| ■ Dark plum #533 | 3 |
| ☐ Light sage #631 | 7 |
| ▦ Dark sage #633 | 8 |
| ☐ Honey gold #645 | 3 |
| ☐ Pale rose #755 | 5 |
| ▦ Cameo rose #759 | 3 |
| ■ New berry #760 | 2 |
| ☐ Light berry #761 | 2 |
| ▦ Windsor blue #808 | 3 |
| ☐ Pale blue #815 | 1 |
| ☐ Country blue #882 | 2 |
| Uncoded areas on door and roof, and around windows are eggshell #111 Continental Stitches | 6 |
| ⁄ Light sage #631 Straight Stitch | |
| ⁄ Dark sage #633 Straight Stitch | |

| Worsted Weight Yarn | Yards |
|---|---|
| ⁄ Honey gold #645 Straight Stitch | |
| ● Bronze #286 French Knot | |
| ◉ Honey gold #645 French Knot | |
| ○ Pale rose #755 French Knot | |
| ○ Country blue #882 French Knot | |
| **#3 Pearl Cotton** | |
| ☐ Very light old gold #677 | 5 |
| Uncoded background on sign cream #712 Continental Stitches | 16 |
| ⁄ Black #310 Backstitch and Straight Stitch | 7 |
| ⁄ Cream #712 Backstitch and Straight Stitch | |
| ○ Very light old gold #677 French Knot | |
| ● Cream #712 French Knot | |
| **#5 Pearl Cotton** | |
| ⁄ Very dark brown gray #3021 Backstitch and Straight Stitch | 20 |
| ● Very dark brown gray #3021 French Knot | |

Color numbers given are for Coats & Clark Red Heart Classic worsted weight yarn Art. E267 and DMC #3 and #5 pearl cotton.

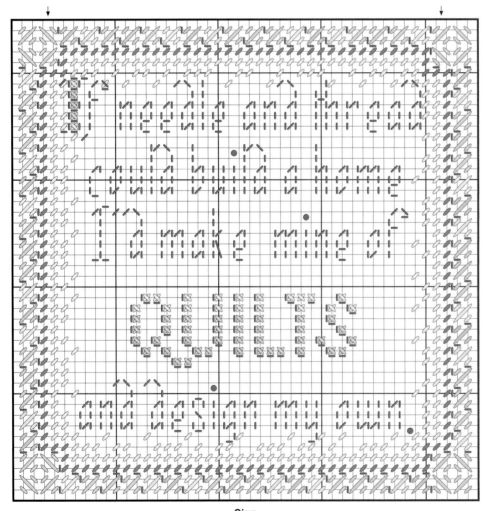

**Sign**
45 holes x 45 holes
Cut 1 from 10-count

**5** Work French Knots on bonnet and dress with very light old gold. Work embroidery at wrist and neckline with very dark brown gray and at top of ladder with black. Do not work remaining black embroidery near bushes at this time.

## Front Wall & Bushes

**1** Using yarn through step 8, work Point Russe #2 Stitch (page 134) on left side of upper windows using colors in following order: dark plum, medium coral, bronze, light sage and honey gold.

**2** Work same stitch on right side of upper windows with colors as follows: dark plum, light sage, dark sage, medium coral and honey gold.

**3** Work border of Point Russe #2 Stitches with Mosaic Checker Stitches using cornmeal and honey gold, and with black and Windsor blue Continental Stitches.

**4** Work Divided Scotch Stitches between top and bottom windows and door with country blue, Windsor blue, warm brown, tan, pale rose and cameo rose. Border these stitches with new berry Continental Stitches.

**5** Work Mosaic Stitches on bottom left side of wall with light berry and dark plum, framing them with Windsor blue Continental Stitches around window and Windsor blue and black Continental Stitches below window.

**6** Repeat step 5 for bottom right side of wall, working Mosaic stitches with black and new berry.

**7** Work bushes with dark sage, light sage, cornmeal and warm brown Continental Stitches.

**8** Overcast walls with Windsor blue, bushes with dark sage and warm brown, and grass edges with dark sage.

## Finishing

**1** Complete embroidery detailing using very dark brown gray and black pearl cotton.

**2** Following steps 3 and 4 under Sunbonnet Sue and ladder, work flowers on bushes with pale rose yarn and very light old gold pearl cotton.

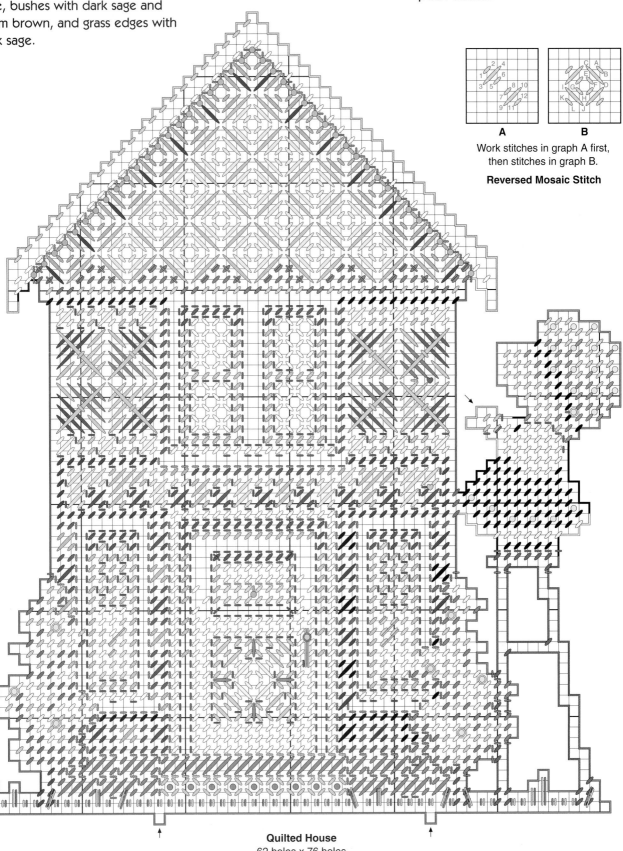

**A**          **B**

Work stitches in graph A first, then stitches in graph B.

**Reversed Mosaic Stitch**

**Quilted House**
62 holes x 76 holes
Cut 1 from 7-count stiff

**3** Straight Stitch grass using a double strand yarn, one strand each light sage and dark sage. Allow yarn to lay as it comes without trying to keep light sage always on one side and dark sage on the other.

**4** For "quilting needle and thread" accent, slide eye pin through Overcast edge of hand where indicated with arrow, keeping eye at bottom.

**5** Work small cream pearl cotton Straight Stitch where indicated in right Point Russe #2 Stitch, then bring needle up through hole indicated with red heart.

**6** Draw pearl cotton through eye of eye pin, then bring back

down through hole indicated with yellow heart, keeping "thread" loose, not tight (see photo); secure on backside. Add a dab of glue to eye to secure arrangement.

**7** Using cream pearl cotton, sew one tulip basket button to each side of the word "QUILT" on sign (see photo). Using floss to match yarn colors, attach sawtooth hanger to back of roof.

**8** Attach house to sign with jump rings where indicated with arrows at bottom of house and top of sign. #

**COLOR KEY**

| Worsted Weight Yarn | Yard |
|---|---|
| ☐ Off-white #3 | |
| ■ Black #12 | |
| ☐ Cornmeal #220 | |
| ▦ Medium coral #252 | |
| ■ Bronze #286 | |
| ▦ Tan #334 | |
| ■ Warm brown #336 | |
| ■ Dark plum #533 | |
| ☐ Light sage #631 | |
| ■ Dark sage #633 | |
| ☐ Honey gold #645 | |
| ☐ Pale rose #755 | |
| ▦ Cameo rose #759 | |
| ■ New berry #760 | |
| ▦ Light berry #761 | |
| ■ Windsor blue #808 | |
| ☐ Pale blue #815 | |
| ☐ Country blue #882 | |

Uncoded areas on door and roof, and around windows are eggshell #111 Continental Stitches
⁄ Light sage #631 Straight Stitch
⁄ Dark sage #633 Straight Stitch
⁄ Honey gold #645 Straight Stitch
● Bronze #286 French Knot
● Honey gold #645 French Knot
○ Pale rose #755 French Knot
○ Country blue #882 French Knot

**#3 Pearl Cotton**
☐ Very light old gold #677
Uncoded background on sign cream #712 Continental Stitches
⁄ Black #310 Backstitch and Straight Stitch
⁄ Cream #712 Backstitch and Straight Stitch
○ Very light old gold #677 French Knot
● Cream #712 French Knot

**#5 Pearl Cotton**
⁄ Very dark brown gray #3021 Backstitch and Straight Stitch
● Very dark brown gray #3021 French Knot

Color numbers given are for Coats & Clark Red Heart Classic worsted weight yarn Art. E267 and DMC #3 and #5 pearl cotton.

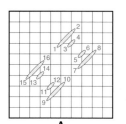

**A**

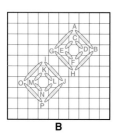

**B**

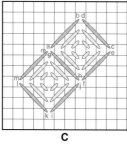

**C**

Using one color, work stitches in graph A first, then stitches in graph B. Using second color, work stitches in graph C last.

**Windowpane Scotch Stitch**

Using one color, first work numbered stitches in order given. Using a second color, work lettered stitches next in order given.

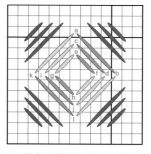

Using third color, work lettered stitches in order given.

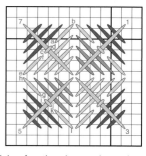

Using fourth color, work numbered stitches in order given, with all stitches meeting in center hole. Using fifth and last color, work lettered stitches in order given, working completely around to first stitch.

**Point Russe #2**

**Native American Patchwork Box continued from page 128** — — — — — — — —

**COLOR KEY**

| Worsted Weight Yarn | Yards |
|---|---|
| ☐ Ivory | 30 |
| ■ Purple | 8 |
| ■ Burgundy | 8 |
| ■ Olive green | 4 |
| Uncoded border on lid is ivory Continental Stitches | |

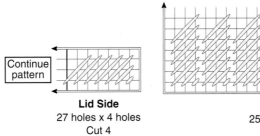

Continue pattern

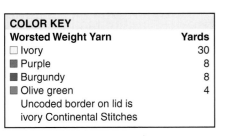

Continue pattern

**Lid Side**
27 holes x 4 holes
Cut 4

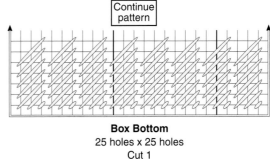

Continue pattern

**Box Bottom**
25 holes x 25 holes
Cut 1

**Flowers on the Square & Good Luck Rainbow continued from page 129** — — — — — — —

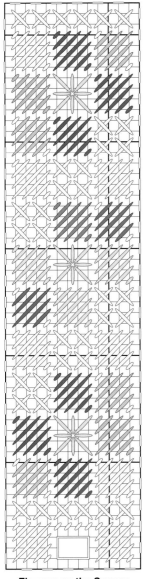

**COLOR KEY**
**Flowers on the Square**

| 6-Strand Embroidery Floss | Yards |
|---|---|
| ☐ White | 6 |
| ■ Dark lavender #209 | 2 |
| ■ Medium lavender #210 | 1 |
| ■ Light cranberry #604 | 1 |
| ■ Kelly green #702 | 1 |
| ■ Bright chartreuse #704 | 1 |
| ☐ Medium light topaz #725 | 1 |
| ☐ Light mauve #3689 | 1 |

Color numbers given are for DMC 6-strand embroidery floss.

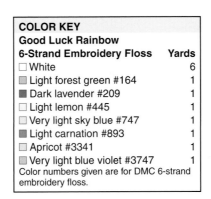

**COLOR KEY**
**Good Luck Rainbow**

| 6-Strand Embroidery Floss | Yards |
|---|---|
| ☐ White | 6 |
| ■ Light forest green #164 | 1 |
| ■ Dark lavender #209 | 1 |
| ☐ Light lemon #445 | 1 |
| ☐ Very light sky blue #747 | 1 |
| ■ Light carnation #893 | 1 |
| ☐ Apricot #3341 | 1 |
| ☐ Very light blue violet #3747 | 1 |

Color numbers given are for DMC 6-strand embroidery floss.

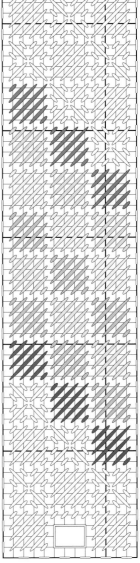

**Flowers on the Square**
13 holes x 53 holes
Cut 1

**Good Luck Rainbow**
13 holes x 53 holes
Cut 1

# Americana Nesting Boxes

Designs by Kristine Loffredo

Let the spirit of Old Glory trumpet in pride when you display
this **patriotic trio** of Stars-and-Stripes boxes!

## Skill Level • Beginner

## Finished Size

**Large Box:** 7³/₈ inches W x
3⁵/₈ inches H x 3⁵/₈ inches D

**Medium Box:** 6¼ inches W x
2⁵/₈ inches H x 2⁵/₈ inches D

**Small Box:** 5¹/₈ inches W x
1⁵/₈ inches H x 1¾ inches D

## Materials

- 2 sheets 7-count plastic canvas
- 6 Uniek QuickShape plastic canvas stars
- Uniek Needloft plastic canvas yarn as listed in color key
- #16 tapestry needle

## Instructions

**1** Cut stars from plastic canvas star shapes (page 139) following graphs, cutting away gray areas.

**2** Cut box and lid pieces from 7-count plastic canvas following graphs (page 138). Cut one 49-hole x 22-hole piece for large box bottom, one 40-hole x 15-hole piece for medium box bottom and one 32-hole x 9-hole piece for small box bottom.

**3** Stitch pieces following graphs, working uncoded areas with red Continental Stitches.

**4** For each box, using red, Whipstitch long sides to short sides, then Whipstitch sides to unstitched bottom; Overcast top edges.

**5** For each lid, using red, Whipstitch long sides to short sides, then Whipstitch sides to top. Overcast bottom edges.

**6** Using photo as a guide, attach stars to lid tops with gold yarn as follows, one each of stars A and B to small lid top; one each of stars B and C to medium lid top; and one each of stars C and D to large lid top. #

| COLOR KEY | |
|---|---|
| **Plastic Canvas Yarn** | **Yards** |
| ■ Red #01 | 119 |
| ☐ Gold #17 | 5 |
| ☐ Eggshell #39 | 11 |
| ■ Dark royal #48 | 5 |
| Uncoded areas are red #01 Continental Stitches | |
| Color numbers given are for Uniek Needloft plastic canvas yarn. | |

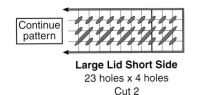

**Large Lid Short Side**
23 holes x 4 holes
Cut 2

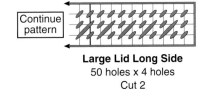

**Large Lid Long Side**
50 holes x 4 holes
Cut 2

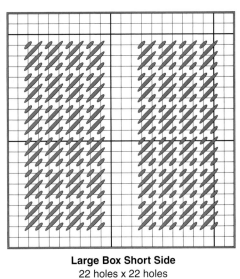

**Large Box Short Side**
22 holes x 22 holes
Cut 2

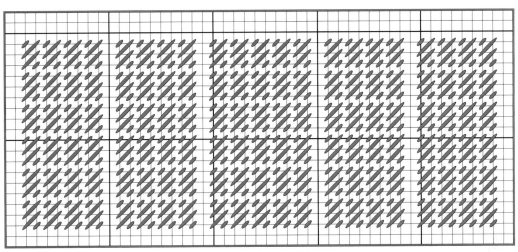

**Large Box Long Side**
49 holes x 22 holes
Cut 2

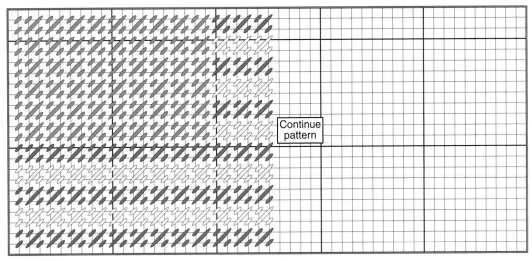

**Large Lid Top**
50 holes x 23 holes
Cut 1

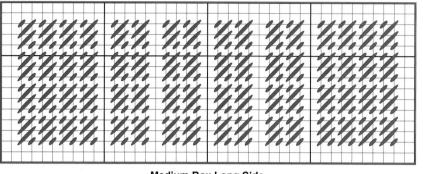

**Medium Box Long Side**
40 holes x 15 holes
Cut 2

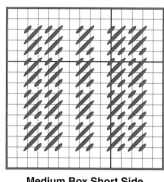

**Medium Box Short Side**
15 holes x 15 holes
Cut 2

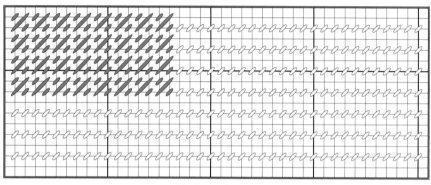

**Medium Lid Top**
41 holes x 16 holes
Cut 1

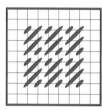

**Small Box Short Side**
9 holes x 9 holes
Cut 2

Continue
pattern

**Medium Lid Long Side**
41 holes x 4 holes
Cut 2

**Small Lid Long Side**
33 holes x 4 holes
Cut 2

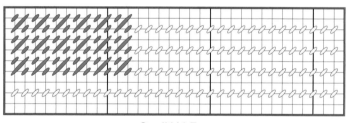

**Small Lid Top**
33 holes x 10 holes
Cut 1

Continue
pattern

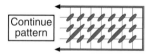

**Medium Lid Short Side**
15 holes x 4 holes
Cut 2

**Small Lid Short Side**
10 holes x 4 holes
Cut 2

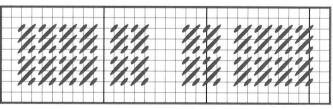

**Small Box Long Side**
32 holes x 9 holes
Cut 2

| COLOR KEY | |
| --- | --- |
| **Plastic Canvas Yarn** | **Yards** |
| ■ Red #01 | 119 |
| ☐ Gold #17 | 5 |
| ☐ Eggshell #39 | 11 |
| ■ Dark royal #48 | 5 |
| Uncoded areas are red | |
| #01 Continental Stitches | |
| Color numbers given are for Uniek Needloft plastic canvas yarn. | |

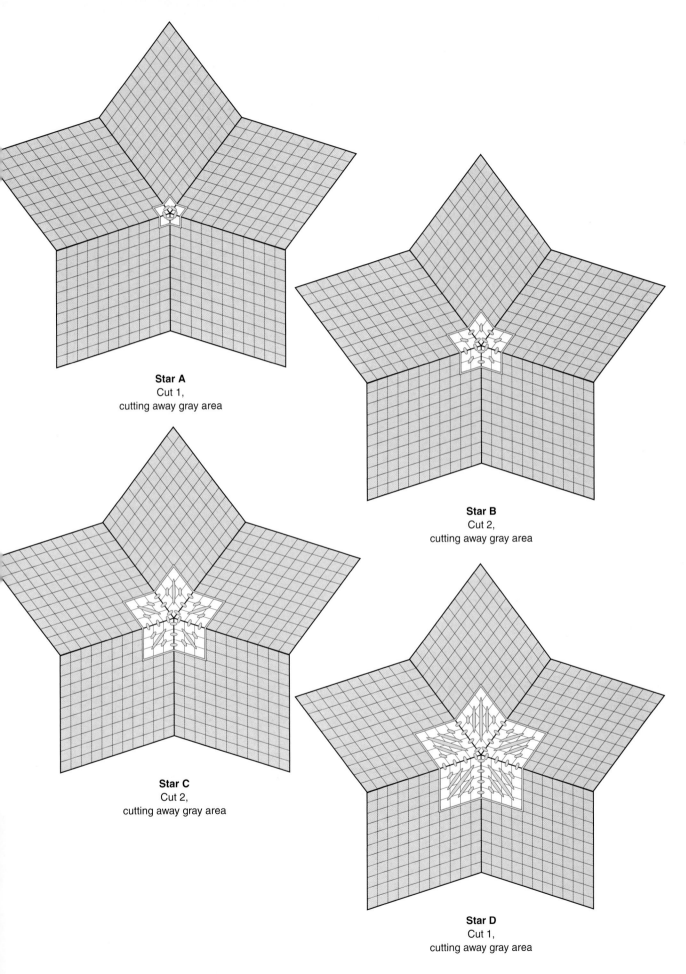

**Star A**
Cut 1,
cutting away gray area

**Star B**
Cut 2,
cutting away gray area

**Star C**
Cut 2,
cutting away gray area

**Star D**
Cut 1,
cutting away gray area

# CHAPTER SEVEN

# Surface Embellishments

Take your stitching to the next level with our charming collection of surface-embroidered designs!

It's easy to spice up plain backgrounds with surface embellishments.

**Backstitch**

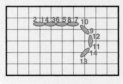

**French Knot**

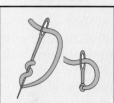

**Lazy Daisy**

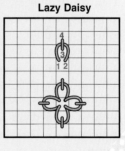

Stitches such as French Knots, Backstitching and Lazy Daisy add a powerful punch to your projects!

# Sewing Notions Box

*Design by Linda Wyszynski*

This **delicate notions box** decorates your table and opens like a flower to safeguard your sewing supplies!

## Skill Level • Intermediate

## Finished Size

3½ inches W x 5⅜ inches H x 3½ inches D

## Materials

- 2 sheets 10-count plastic canvas
- DMC #3 pearl cotton as listed in color key
- DMC 6-strand embroidery floss as listed in color key
- Kreinik Medium (#16) Braid as listed in color key
- #20 tapestry needle
- ⅞-inch x 1-inch antique gold basket charm #AG1134 from Creative Beginnings
- White felt
- 28 inches ⅝-inch-wide white grosgrain ribbon with gold strips
- ¼ yard white moire fabric
- Quilt batting
- Craft and quilting fleece
- 2¼-inch-square x 1-inch-thick piece plastic foam
- 11-inch x 17-inch PeelnStick adhesive sheet by Therm O Web
- Hand-sewing needle
- White sewing thread
- 1 yard 4-pound fishing line
- Straight pins
- Jewel glue

## Cutting

**1** Cut plastic canvas according to graphs (pages 143 and 151).

**2** Cut one 24-hole x 24-hole piece for pincushion shell base and four 29-hole x 47-hole pieces for box side liners. Pincushion shell base, four box liners and one box bottom will remain unstitched.

**3** Cut one 3⅜-inch square white felt for lid liner. Cut four pieces each of felt and fleece, and eight pieces of adhesive sheet to fit box side liners. Cut four 4-inch x 6-inch pieces of white moire fabric.

**4** Cut four 2¼-inch squares of quilt batting.

## Box Sides & Bottom

**1** Stitch box sides following graphs, working Van Dyke Stitches (page 151) with white.

**2** Stitch one box bottom following graph, working only the portion indicated, leaving center area unstitched.

**3** When background stitching is completed, work gold braid Straight Stitches. Work bronze braid Straight Stitches at top of center section on each side.

**4** Using 4 plies floss, randomly place French Knot flowers and leaves in a hanging basket shape, working one color at a time (see photo). Use green shades for

leaves; use remaining colors for flowers. While working flowers and leaves, keep in mind there are seven colors to place.

**5** Overcast top and side edges of box sides, leaving bottom edges unworked. Do not Whipstitch sides together.

## Box Lid

**1** Following graphs, stitch box lid top and sides, working Van Dyke Stitches with white.

**2** When background stitching is completed, work dark delft blue Backstitches and gold braid Straight Stitches on lid top.

**3** Using fishing line, attach basket charm to center of box lid top. Work French Knot flowers and leaves around basket rim and handle in a floral arrangement (see photo), using 4 plies floss in same colors used in step 4 under box sides and bottom.

**4** Using white, Whipstitch sides together, then Whipstitch sides to top; Overcast bottom edges of sides. Glue felt square to wrong side of lid top.

## Box Side Liners

**1** For each liner, use adhesive sheet to attach felt to one side and fleece to other side.

**2** Cover fleece side with moire fabric, pulling fabric tightly around canvas over edges to felt side; secure with small strips of adhesive sheet.

**3** Miter corners and trim fabric as needed. Cut four 4-inch lengths white grosgrain ribbon. Wrap a length around center of each section of moire, gluing ends to felt side.

**4** For each side, place felt side of one liner next to backside of one box side; stitch in place using hand-sewing needle and white sewing thread.

## Pincushion Shell

**1** Stitch shell sides following graph. Using pale delft blue, Whipstitch sides together, then Whipstitch sides to unstitched shell base; Overcast top edges.

**2** Using hand-sewing needle and white sewing thread, attach remaining length of grosgrain ribbon around top of sides, overlapping ends and turning under top edge.

**3** Center shell over stitch bottom. Using white pearl cotton and several large stitches inside the box, sew shell base to stitched bottom.

**4** If needed, trim plastic foam to fit inside shell. Trim quilt batting as necessary to fit on top of plastic foam. Glue together; let dry.

**5** Cover plastic foam and batting with moire fabric; glue in place. Use straight pins to hold in place until dry.

**6** Place covered plastic foam inside shell, securing with a small amount of glue inside shell walls. Use straight pins to hold sides and pincushion together until dry.

## Final Assembly

**1** Place bottom pieces together, then use white to Whipstitch bottom pieces to bottom edges of sides, working through all three thicknesses.

**2** To close box, lift up sides, then place lid on top over sides. #

| COLOR KEY | |
|---|---|
| **#3 Pearl Cotton** | **Yards** |
| □ White | 32 |
| ■ Dark delft blue #798 | 16 |
| □ Pale delft blue #800 | 16 |
| ⁄ Dark delft blue #798 Backstitch | |
| **Medium (#16) Braid** | |
| □ Gold #002 | 22 |
| ⁄ Gold #002 Straight Stitch | |
| ⁄ Bronze hi lustre | |
| #052HL Straight Stitch | 2 |
| **6-Strand Embroidery Floss** | |
| Very dark lavender #208 French Knot | 2 |
| Light lemon #445 French Knot | 2 |
| Very dark blue green #500 French Knot | 2 |
| Dark garnet #814 French Knot | 2 |
| Dark sea green #958 French Knot | 2 |
| Dark celadon green #3815 French Knot | 2 |
| Dark straw #3821 French Knot | 2 |
| Color numbers given are for DMC #3 pearl cotton and 6-strand embroidery floss, and Kreinik Medium (#16) Braid. | |

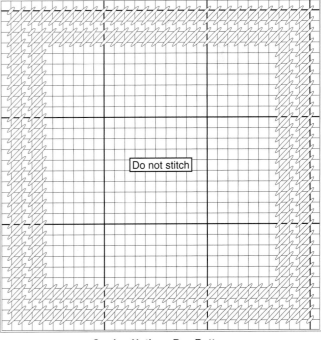

**Sewing Notions Box Bottom**
31 holes x 31 holes
Cut 2, stitch 1

Do not stitch

# Golden Vines Picture Frame

*Design by Ruby Thacker*

This **magnificent ivory-and-gold frame** is perfect for brightening your home on any number of special occasions!

## Skill Level • Intermediate

## Finished Size

6⅜ inches W x 8¼ inches H

## Materials

- 1 sheet stiff 7-count plastic canvas
- Uniek Needloft yarn as listed in color key
- DMC 6-strand metallic embroidery floss as listed in color key
- #16 tapestry needle
- 12 (3mm) gold beads

## Instructions

**1** Cut plastic canvas according to graphs, cutting out all nine openings on front and opening for hanger on back. Frame back will remain unstitched.

**2** Work uncoded background on frame front with white Continental Stitches, leaving areas indicated with blue highlighted Whipstitch lines unworked at this time; Overcast photo opening.

**3** Using 6 plies gold metallic embroidery floss, work Cross Stitches and Overcast outer areas on frame front.

**4** Using 3 plies gold metallic floss, work Backstitches and Lazy Daisy Stitches over white Continental Stitches.

**5** Using 1 ply gold metallic floss, attach gold beads to center of flowers where indicated in graph.

**6** Matching corner edges of frames, Whipstitch frame front and back together with white, using Continental Stitches to Whipstitch front to back at blue lines, then Overcast remaining edges of frame front. #

| COLOR KEY | |
|---|---|
| **Plastic Canvas Yarn** | **Yards** |
| Uncoded areas are white #41 Continental Stitches | 17 |
| ⁄ White #41 Overcasting and Whipstitching | |
| **6-Strand Metallic Embroidery Floss** | |
| ☐ Gold #5282 | 12 |
| ⁄ Gold #5282 Backstitch | |
| ◖ Gold #5282 Lazy Daisy Stitch | |
| ● Attach gold bead | |
| Color numbers given are for Uniek Needloft plastic canvas yarn and DMC 6-strand metallic embroidery floss. | |

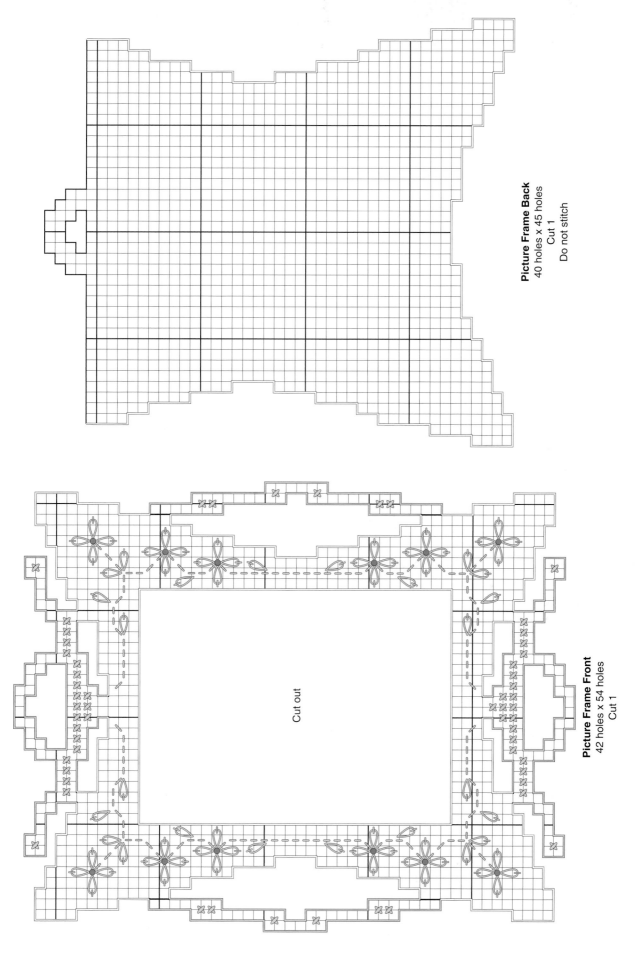

**Picture Frame Back**
40 holes x 45 holes
Cut 1
Do not stitch

**Picture Frame Front**
42 holes x 54 holes
Cut 1

Cut out

# Spring Flowers Stocking

Design by Janna Britton

Any day can be a happy holiday when you hang
this bright and cheerful floral stocking!

## Skill Level • Intermediate

### Finished Size

4⅝ inches W x 7¼ inches H, excluding hanger

## Materials

- 1 sheet 7-count plastic canvas
- Uniek Needloft plastic canvas yarn as listed in color key
- 6-strand embroidery floss as listed in color key
- #16 tapestry needle

## Instructions

**1** Cut two stockings from plastic canvas according to graph.

**2** Stitch background on pieces following graph, reversing back before stitching and working uncoded areas with watermelon Continental Stitches.

**3** When background stitching is completed, work Cross Stitches with 6 plies white floss on both front and back.

**4** Work remaining embroidery on stocking front only. Work each white yarn flower with a Ridged Spiderweb Stitch, wrapping yarn tightly, but not enough to distort spokes.

**5** Using moss, work Lazy Daisy Stitches and Straight Stitches, then work yellow French Knots, wrapping yarn two times around needle.

**6** Work a row of white yarn Turkey Loop Stitches at bottom of cuff were indicated with blue line.

**7** Overcast top edges of stocking with white.

Whipstitch front and back together with white, watermelon and yellow.

**8** For hanger, thread desired length of white yarn through stitches at inside back seam. Knot ends together inside stocking. #

**COLOR KEY**

| Plastic Canvas Yarn | Yards |
|---|---|
| ☐ White #41 | 10 |
| ☐ Yellow #57 | 5 |
| Uncoded area is watermelon #55 Continental Stitches | 25 |
| ✎ Watermelon #55 Whipstitching | |
| ✎ Moss #25 Straight Stitch | 2 |
| ✎ White #41 Ridged Spiderweb Stitch | |
| ⟋ Moss #25 Lazy Daisy Stitch | |
| ○ Yellow #57 French Knot | |
| **6-Strand Embroidery Floss** | |
| ✕ White Cross Stitch | 3 |

Color numbers given are for Uniek Needloft plastic canvas yarn.

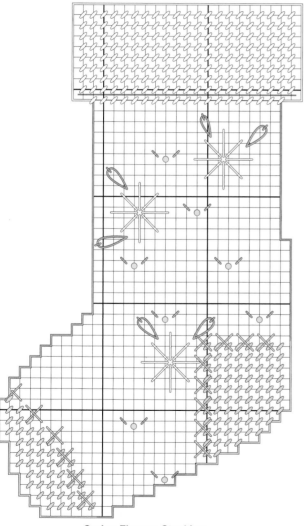

**Spring Flowers Stocking**
29 holes x 48 holes
Cut 2, reverse 1

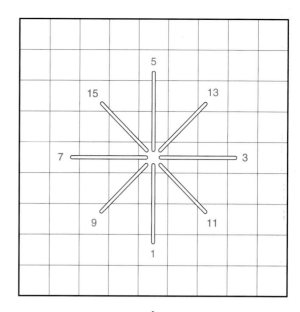

**A**
Straight Stitch spokes as
in graph A first, with
stitches meeting in center.

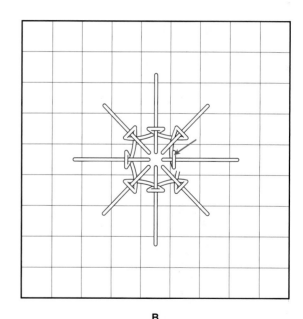

**B**
Following graph B, bring
needle up close to center hole
(indicated with red arrow).
Take yarn over one spoke,
wrap under two spokes, back
over one spoke, under two, etc.
Complete one round, then work three
more rounds for a total of four rounds.

**Ridged Spiderweb Stitch**

# Holly Angel

*Design by Maryanne Moreck*

Deck the mantel with this sweet Christmas angel, all dressed up in her holly-jolly best!

## Skill Level • Intermediate

## Finished Size

6⅞ inches W x 6⅞ inches H x 7 inches D, excluding halo

## Materials

- 2 sheets 7-count plastic canvas
- Worsted weight yarn as listed in color key
- ⅛ inch-wide Plastic Canvas 7 Metallic Needlepoint Yarn by Rainbow Gallery as listed in color key
- #16 tapestry needle
- 70 (3mm) gold beads
- Hand-sewing needle
- White sewing thread
- Gold tinsel stem
- White adhesive-backed felt (optional)
- Seam sealant
- Hot-glue gun

## Instructions

**1** Cut pieces from plastic canvas according to graphs (pages 149 and 150).

**2** Following graphs through step 7, stitch angel following graph, working uncoded area on face with peach Continental Stitches. Overlap shaded blue areas and work stitches indicated.

**3** Overcast edges and work pink Backstitches for mouth. Using hand-sewing needle and white sewing thread, attach gold beads to robe front where indicated on graph.

**4** Stitch cape, working uncoded areas with white Continental Stitches. Join corners at arrows with a white Whipstitch. Slip cape over angel's head.

**5** Stitch and Overcast wings, leaving area indicated unstitched. Attach beads where indicated with hand-sewing needle and white sewing thread.

**6** If desired, cut felt to fit wings and adhere to backside. Insert unstitched portion of wings in hole behind head.

**7** Stitch and Overcast holly leaves. Work green Straight Stitch down center of each leaf; work deep red French Knots for holly berries.

**8** Using photo as a guide, glue leaves to front of cape. Tie a length of gold metallic plastic canvas in a bow. Apply seam sealant to ends to prevent fraying. Center and glue bow just under chin.

**9** Form gold tinsel stem into a halo. Place long stem in hole behind head, then attach to back of head with a small amount of glue. #

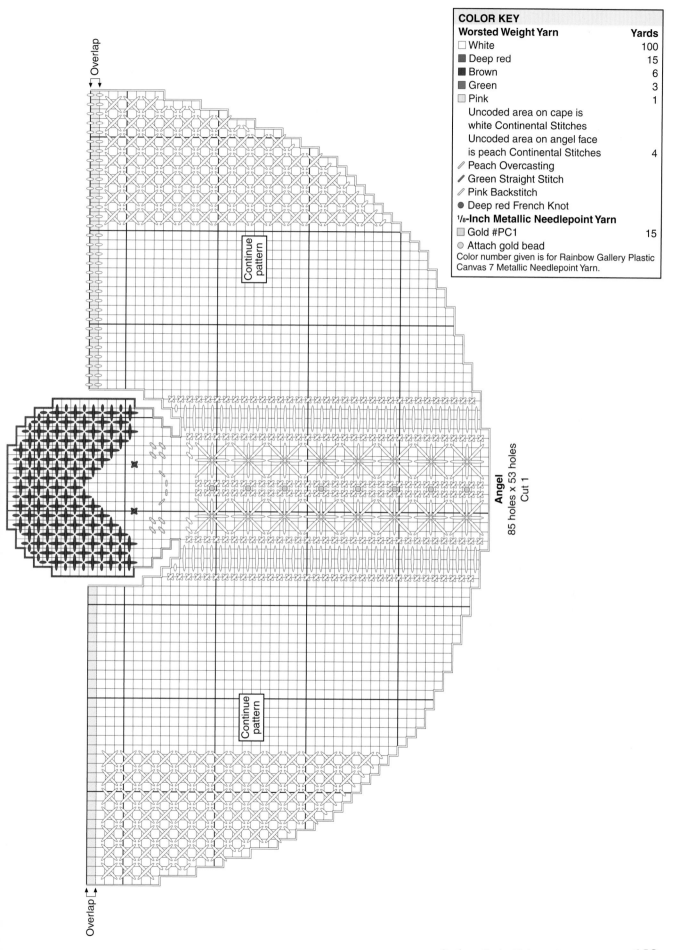

**COLOR KEY**

| Worsted Weight Yarn | Yards |
|---|---|
| ☐ White | 100 |
| ■ Deep red | 15 |
| ■ Brown | 6 |
| ■ Green | 3 |
| ☐ Pink | 1 |
| Uncoded area on cape is white Continental Stitches | |
| Uncoded area on angel face is peach Continental Stitches | 4 |
| ⁄ Peach Overcasting | |
| ⁄ Green Straight Stitch | |
| ⁄ Pink Backstitch | |
| ● Deep red French Knot | |
| **⅛-Inch Metallic Needlepoint Yarn** | |
| ☐ Gold #PC1 | 15 |
| ◯ Attach gold bead | |

Color number given is for Rainbow Gallery Plastic Canvas 7 Metallic Needlepoint Yarn.

Overlap

Continue pattern

Continue pattern

**Angel**
85 holes x 53 holes
Cut 1

Overlap

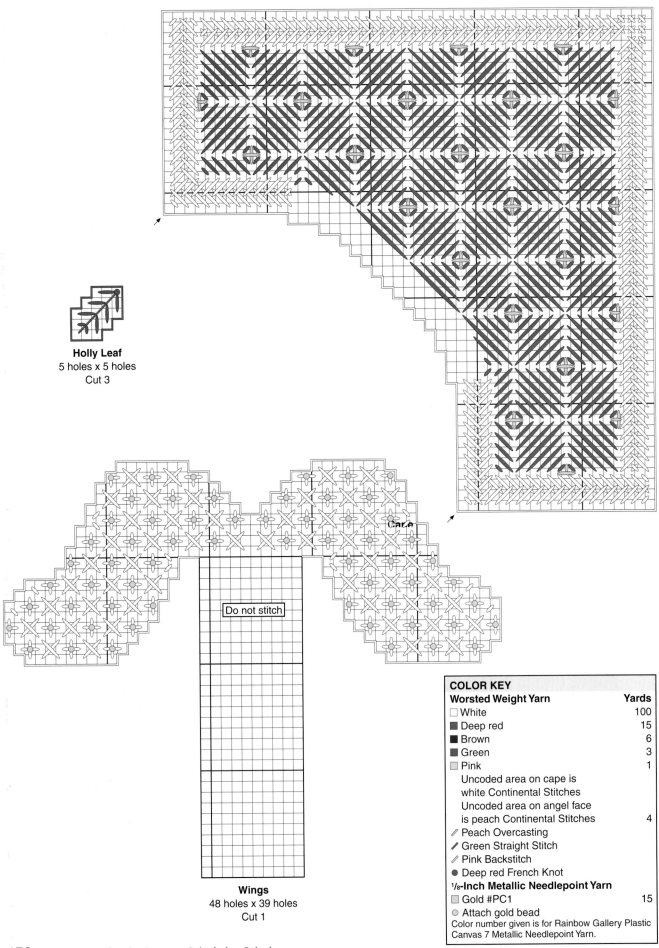

**Holly Leaf**
5 holes x 5 holes
Cut 3

Cape

Do not stitch

**Wings**
48 holes x 39 holes
Cut 1

**COLOR KEY**

| Worsted Weight Yarn | Yards |
|---|---|
| ☐ White | 100 |
| ■ Deep red | 15 |
| ■ Brown | 6 |
| ■ Green | 3 |
| ☐ Pink | 1 |
| Uncoded area on cape is white Continental Stitches | |
| Uncoded area on angel face is peach Continental Stitches | 4 |
| ⁄ Peach Overcasting | |
| ⁄ Green Straight Stitch | |
| ⁄ Pink Backstitch | |
| ● Deep red French Knot | |
| **¹⁄₈-Inch Metallic Needlepoint Yarn** | |
| ☐ Gold #PC1 | 15 |
| ◯ Attach gold bead | |

Color number given is for Rainbow Gallery Plastic Canvas 7 Metallic Needlepoint Yarn.

Sewing Notions Box continued from page 143

**COLOR KEY**

| #3 Pearl Cotton | Yards |
|---|---|
| ☐ White | 32 |
| ▨ Dark delft blue #798 | 16 |
| ☐ Pale delft blue #800 | 16 |
| ⁄ Dark delft blue #798 Backstitch | |

**Medium (#16) Braid**

| | |
|---|---|
| ☐ Gold #002 | 22 |
| ⁄ Gold #002 Straight Stitch | |
| ⁄ Bronze hi lustre | |
| #052HL Straight Stitch | 2 |

**6-Strand Embroidery Floss**

| | |
|---|---|
| Very dark lavender #208 French Knot | 2 |
| Light lemon #445 French Knot | 2 |
| Very dark blue green #500 French Knot | 2 |
| Dark garnet #814 French Knot | 2 |
| Dark sea green #958 French Knot | 2 |
| Dark celadon green #3815 French Knot | 2 |
| Dark straw #3821 French Knot | 2 |

Color numbers given are for DMC #3 pearl cotton and 6-strand embroidery floss, and Kreinik Medium (#16) Braid.

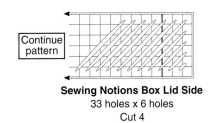

**Sewing Notions Box Lid Side**
33 holes x 6 holes
Cut 4

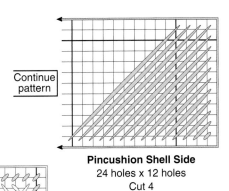

**Pincushion Shell Side**
24 holes x 12 holes
Cut 4

Work stitches in order given, coming up at 1, going down at 2, up at 3, down at 4, etc.

**Van Dyke Stitch**

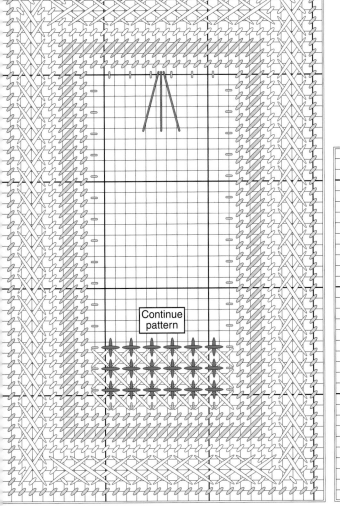

**Sewing Notions Box Side**
31 holes x 49 holes
Cut 4

**Sewing Notions Box Lid Top**
33 holes x 33 holes
Cut 1

# Midnight Blossoms Keepsake Box

Design by Alida Macor

With the quiet glow of beautiful blossoms, this lovely box guards your favorite treasures in serene tranquility!

## Skill Level • Beginner

## Finished Size

5¼ inches W x 1⅞ inches H x 3⅜ inches D

## Materials

- 1 sheet black 7-count plastic canvas
- Worsted weight yarn as listed in color key
- DMC #3 pearl cotton as listed in color key
- #16 tapestry needle
- Black self-adhesive felt

## Instructions

**1** Cut lid pieces from plastic canvas according to graphs (page 155). Cut black felt one hole smaller all around than lid top.

**2** Cut one 31-hole x 19-hole piece for box bottom, two 31-hole x 10-hole pieces for box long sides and two 19-hole x 10-hole pieces for box short sides. Box bottom and sides will remain unstitched.

**3** Stitch lid sides following graphs. Work Ridged Spiderweb Stitch (page 147) on lid top first, Straight Stitching spokes with baby pink.

**4** Work first two rounds with mauve and remaining rounds with baby pink, working as many rounds as needed to cover spokes. **Note:** As the ridges are built, the stitches will be seen between spokes.

**5** Cross Stitch light parrot green leaves next, then work uncoded areas with black Continental Stitches. Work baby pink Cross stitches for border last.

**6** When background stitching is completed, work light parrot green Backstitches and white, medium yellow and medium electric blue French Knots for remaining flowers and leaves.

**7** Adhere felt to wrong side of lid top. Using black through step 8, Whipstitch lid long sides to lid short sides, then Whipstitch sides to lid top; Overcast bottom edges of lid sides.

**8** Whipstitch box long sides to box short sides, then Whipstitch sides to bottom; Overcast top edges of sides. #

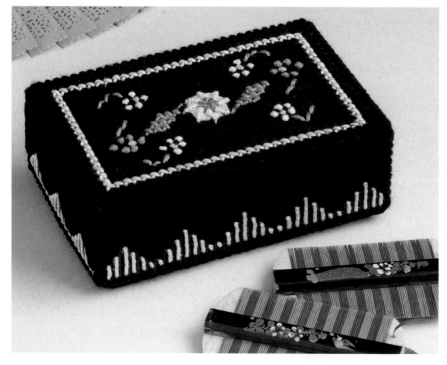

# Victorian Elegance Key Minder

Design by Janelle Giese

This elegant key keeper brings **stately beauty** to your foyer or hallway, combining perfect form with practical function!

## Skill Level • Advanced

### Finished Size

13 inches W x 9⅞ inches H, excluding tassels

### Project Notes

Use a double strand of chenille yarn throughout stitching, working with direction of nap.

By using over-dyed chenille yarn for diamond pattern, each stitched piece will be unique.

# Materials

- 2 sheets 7-count plastic canvas
- Elmore-Pisgah Honeysuckle rayon chenille yarn as listed in color key
- Kreinik Medium (#16) Braid as listed in color key
- 3 yards Kreinik gold #002 Very Fine (#4) Braid
- 1 yard Kreinik antique gold Facets
- 6-strand embroidery floss or thread to match rose yarn
- #16 tapestry needle
- 3-inch drapery hook
- Metallic gold spray paint
- 2 (3-inch) beige tassels
- Sawtooth hanger

## Instructions

**1** Spray hook with metallic gold paint. Allow to dry thoroughly before proceeding.

**2** Cut two key minders from plastic canvas according to graph, cutting out opening for drapery hook in front piece only.

**3** Place two plastic canvas pieces together, making sure piece with opening for drapery hook is on top. Insert hook into hole so it

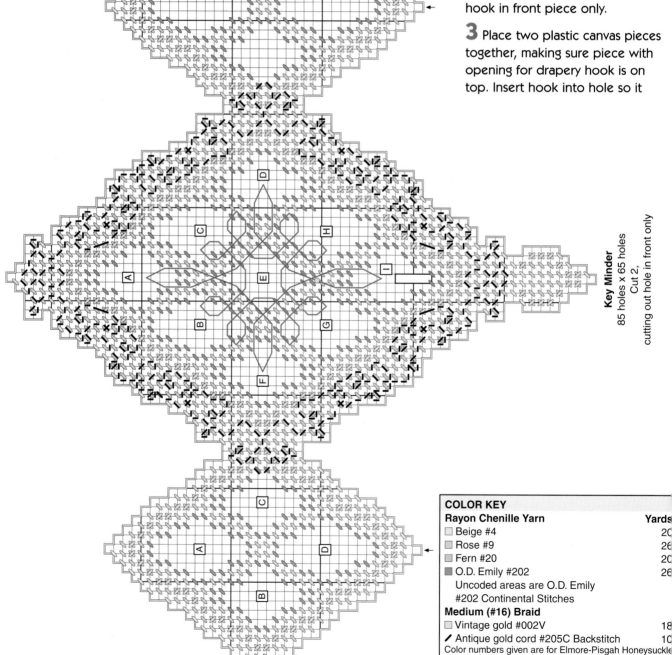

**Key Minder**
85 holes x 65 holes
Cut 2,
cutting out hole in front only

| COLOR KEY | |
|---|---|
| **Rayon Chenille Yarn** | **Yards** |
| ☐ Beige #4 | 20 |
| ☐ Rose #9 | 26 |
| ☐ Fern #20 | 20 |
| ■ O.D. Emily #202 | 26 |
| Uncoded areas are O.D. Emily #202 Continental Stitches | |
| **Medium (#16) Braid** | |
| ☐ Vintage gold #002V | 18 |
| ✦ Antique gold cord #205C Backstitch | 10 |
| Color numbers given are for Elmore-Pisgah Honeysuckle rayon chenille yarn and Kreinik Medium (#16) Braid. | |

is encased between layers before stitching bottom part. Stitching will be worked through both layers and over areas of hook encased between layers.

**4** Following graph, work borders beginning with rose yarn, then using two strands vintage gold. Work all fern stitches next, including borders for center diamonds.

**5** To prepare for O.D. Emily borders, place 1 yard length of same color shades together. Stitch these "inside" borders (indicated with lavender Continental Stitches on graph) one diamond at a time. *Note: Not every diamond border will have the same over-dyed yarn shade.*

**6** Fill in diamond sections in alphabetical order using O.D. Emily as it comes off the ball so stitching will create a watercolor effect. Using beige yarn, complete stitches along edges and Overcast.

**7** When background stitching and Overcasting are completed, Backstitch around center motif with antique gold medium (#16) braid.

**8** Using antique gold facets as laid thread, and gold very fine (#4) braid for couching thread, work center embellishment to motif, following red line for first journey and green line for second journey. Begin and exit couching for first and second journeys at yellow dots.

**9** Using floss to match rose yarn, attach sawtooth hanger to top center backside. Tack tassel loops to back of motif where indicated with arrows, allowing tassels to hang directly below edges. #

**Midnight Blossoms Keepsake Box** continued from page 152 — — — — — — —

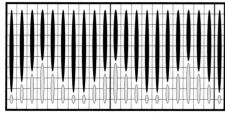

**Lid Short Side**
21 holes x 10 holes
Cut 2

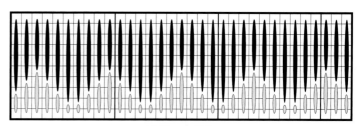

**Lid Long Side**
33 holes x 10 holes
Cut 2

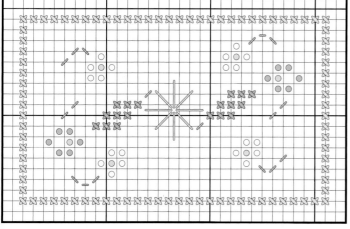

**Lid Top**
33 holes x 21 holes
Cut 1

| COLOR KEY | |
|---|---|
| **Worsted Weight Yarn** | **Yards** |
| ■ Black | 26 |
| Uncoded areas are black | |
| Continental Stitches | |
| **#3 Pearl Cotton** | |
| □ Baby pink #818 | 7 |
| ▨ Light parrot green #907 | 2 |
| ⁄ Baby pink #818 Straight Stitch | |
| ⁄ Light parrot green | |
| #907 Straight Stitch | |
| Mauve #3687 Ridged | 1 |
| Spiderweb Stitch | 1 |
| ○ White French Knot | 1 |
| ○ Medium yellow #743 French Knot | |
| ● Medium electric blue | 1 |
| #996 French Knot | |
| Color numbers given are for DMC #3 pearl cotton. | |

# CHAPTER EIGHT

# Fancy Joining Stitches

## Overcasting never looked so good and was never so much fun!

When your plastic canvas pieces have been lovingly stitched and beautifully embellished, it's time

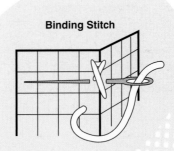

**Binding Stitch**

for the crowning moment—joining them together! Watch your project take creative shape with our superb selection of innovative designs, each of which makes use of fun and fancy joining stitches!

# Black Elegance Frame & Box Set

*Designs by Angie Arickx*

For evening entertaining or formal festivities, this stunning set is sure to enhance the occasion!

## Skill Level • Beginner

### Finished Size

**Frame:** 9½ inches W x 7¼ inches H x 1¾ inches D

**Box:** 3½ inches W x 2¾ inches H x 3½ inches D

## Materials

- 1 sheet 7-count plastic canvas
- Uniek Needloft plastic canvas yarn as listed in color key
- Uniek Needloft metallic craft cord as listed in color key
- #16 tapestry needle
- Double 5-inch x 7-inch acrylic photo frame
- PeelnStick double-sided adhesive by Therm O Web
- Black felt (optional)
- Hot-glue gun

## Instructions

**1** Cut plastic canvas according to graphs. (this page and page 163). Cut one 23-hole x 23-hole piece for box bottom; leave unstitched.

**2** Stitch pieces following graphs. Using alternating colors of black and solid gold, Overcast outside edges of lid top, top edges of box sides, and inside and outside edges of frames. Overcast lid bottom with black.

**3** Using black, Whipstitch box sides together, then Whipstitch sides to unstitched box bottom.

**4** Using solid gold, Whipstitch knob sides together, then Whipstitch knob sides to knob top; Whipstitch assembled knob to inside edges of box top.

**5** Using strips of double-sided adhesive, attach stitched frames to acrylic photo frame with ¾-inch-wide strips along top and bottom, ¼-inch strips along the sides and a 1½-inch strip in the center. Make each strip long enough to cover width of frame at top and bottom, and length of frame at sides. Butt edges of frames together in the center.

**6** With wrong sides facing, center lid bottom under lid top; glue together. #

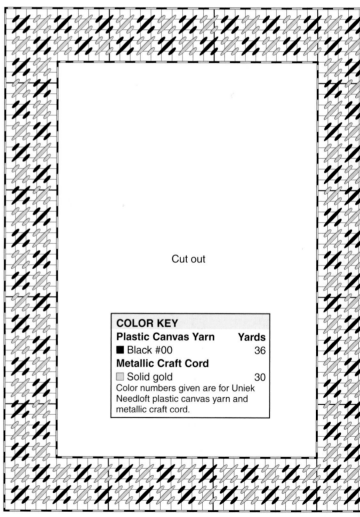

> **COLOR KEY**
>
> | Plastic Canvas Yarn | Yards |
> |---|---|
> | ■ Black #00 | 36 |
> | **Metallic Craft Cord** | |
> | ☐ Solid gold | 30 |
>
> Color numbers given are for Uniek Needloft plastic canvas yarn and metallic craft cord.

Cut out

**Frame**
35 holes x 47 holes
Cut 2

# Fancy Flower Fridgies

Designs by Vicki Blizzard

Hold your favorite photos in style
with these fancy little magnets featuring two-color Overcasting.

## Skill Level • Beginner

### Finished Size

Approximately 2³⁄₈ inches square x
⁵⁄₈ inches D

### Materials

- ½ sheet 7-count plastic canvas
- Uniek Needloft plastic canvas yarn as listed in color key
- #16 tapestry needle
- 6 (2-inch) lengths magnet strip
- Hot-glue gun

### Instructions

**1** Cut and stitch plastic canvas according to graphs (page 161).

**2** Following graphs throughout, stitch and Overcast flowers. Work yellow French Knots on all geraniums, the bachelor button and one painted daisy.

**3** Stitch magnet bases following graph, working uncoded area on each with white Continental Stitches.

**4** Using fern and beginning in corner with three stitches, work Overcast in every other hole, working three stitches in each remaining corner. Overcast remaining holes with white.

**5** Center and glue bachelor's button to front of one base.

**6** Center and glue painted daisy piece without French Knots to front of one base. Glue daisy piece with French Knots on top, placing petals between petals of first layer.

**7** Glue four geraniums to front of remaining base. Center and glue remaining flower on top.

**8** Glue two magnet strips to back of each base. #

# Color Blocks Tissue Topper

*Design by Angie Arickx*

You'll love the subtle optical illusions and pleasant pastels of this innovative tissue topper!

## Skill Level • Intermediate

### Finished Size

Fits boutique-style tissue box

### Materials

- 1¼ sheets 7-count plastic canvas
- Uniek Needloft plastic canvas yarn as listed in color key
- #16 tapestry needle

### Instructions

**1** Cut and stitch plastic canvas according to graphs.

**2** Using white through step 3, Overcast bottom edges of sides and inside edges of top with a Modified Herringbone Overcast Stitch, skipping every other hole for a stretched-out look.

**3** Whipstitch sides A to sides B, then Whipstitch sides to top with a modified Cross Stitch, skipping every other hole and matching colors on top to colors on sides. #

| COLOR KEY | |
|---|---|
| **Plastic Canvas Yarn** | **Yards** |
| ☐ White #41 | 38 |
| ☐ Orchid #44 | 28 |
| ☐ Lilac #45 | 28 |
| Color numbers given are for Uniek Needloft plastic canvas yarn. | |

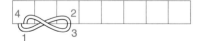

Bring needle up at 1, over the edge and down at 2, up at 3 and down at 4.

Bring needle under edge and up at 5, down at 6, up at 7 and down at 8.

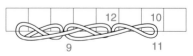

Bring needle under edge, around yarn and up at 9, down at 10, up at 11 and down at 12. Continue until edge is covered.

**Modified Herringbone Overcast Stitch**

**Topper Side A**
31 holes x 37 holes
Cut 2

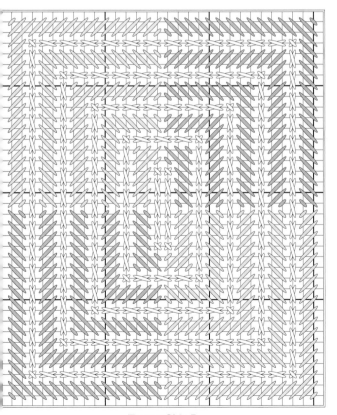

**Topper Side B**
31 holes x 37 holes
Cut 2

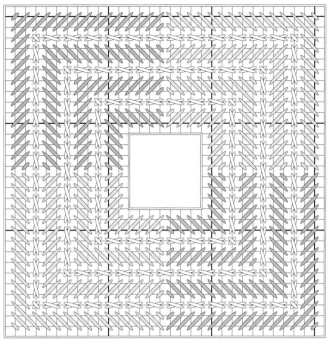

**Topper Top**
31 holes x 31 holes
Cut 1

**Fancy Flower Fridgies continued from page 159** ──

**Painted Daisy**
11 holes x 11 holes
Cut 2
Work French Knots
on 1 piece only

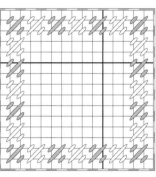

**Magnet Base**
15 holes x 15 holes
Cut 3

**Geranium**
5 holes x 5 holes
Cut 5

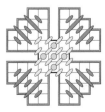

**Bachelor's Button**
9 holes x 9 holes
Cut 1

| COLOR KEY | |
|---|---|
| **Plastic Canvas Yarn** | **Yards** |
| ■ Christmas red #02 | 5 |
| ☐ Pink #07 | 3 |
| ☐ Fern #23 | 8 |
| ■ Sail blue #35 | 1 |
| ☐ Baby blue #36 | 1 |
| ☐ White #41 | 15 |
| Uncoded areas are white | |
| #41 Continental Stitches | |
| ○ Yellow #57 French Knot | 3 |
| Color numbers given are for Uniek | |
| Needloft plastic canvas yarn. | |

# Vase of Flowers Bookmark

Design by Kathy Wirth

Hold your place in your latest reading material with a bookmark reminiscent of a painted still life. Two-color Overcasting adds colorful style!

## Skill Level • Beginner

To anchor first stitch of each length, pass needle through loop on back and pull taut. Make sure all stitches are laid smoothly and strands are untwisted.

## Instructions

**1** Cut plastic canvas according to graph.

**2** Stitch piece following graph, working uncoded background with ice blue Continental Stitches.

**3** When background stitching is completed, work Lazy Daisy Stitches for bottom flower and French Knots for flower centers.

**4** Overcast edges using alternating colors of black and white. #

## Finished Size

2¼ inches W x 6¾ inches L

## Materials

- ¼ sheet clear 10-count plastic canvas
- Coats & Clark Anchor 6-strand embroidery floss as listed in color key
- #20 tapestry needle

## Project Notes

Work entire project with a double strand (12 plies) floss.

Cut five 1¾-yard lengths of floss per skein. Fold each length in half, matching cut ends. Thread cut ends through eye of needle, leaving a loop at other end. For easier threading, fold small piece of paper over cut ends and insert into eye.

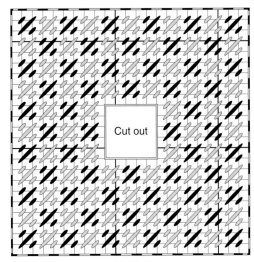

**Lid Top**
23 holes x 23 holes
Cut 1

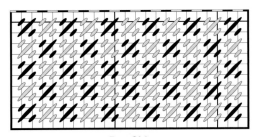

**Box Side**
23 holes x 11 holes
Cut 4

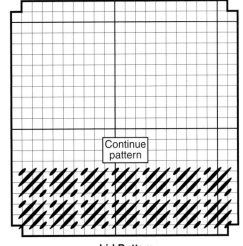

**Lid Bottom**
22 holes x 22 holes
Cut 1

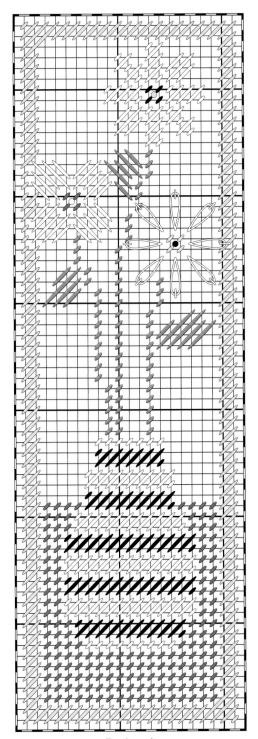

**Bookmark**
22 holes x 67 holes
Cut 1

**Knob Top**
5 holes x 5 holes
Cut 1

**Knob Side**
5 holes x 3 holes
Cut 4

| COLOR KEY | |
|---|---|
| **Plastic Canvas Yarn** | **Yards** |
| ■ Black #00 | 36 |
| **Metallic Craft Cord** | |
| ▨ Solid gold | 30 |
| Color numbers given are for Uniek Needloft plastic canvas yarn and metallic craft cord. | |

# Antique Shoppe Tissue Topper

Design by Nancy Dorman

Quaint and beautifully detailed, this charming tissue topper will
whisk you away to a historic town square!

## Skill Level • Intermediate

### Finished Size

Fits boutique-style tissue box

## Materials

- 3 sheets 7-count plastic canvas
- ¼ sheet clear 10-count plastic canvas
- Small amount black 10-count plastic canvas
- Worsted weight yarn as listed in color key
- Sport weight yarn as listed in color key
- 6-strand embroidery floss as listed in color key
- Medium metallic braid as listed in color key
- #16 tapestry needle
- #18 tapestry needle
- 1-inch tan flocked teddy bear
- ⅜-inch gold liberty bell
- ½-inch-diameter miniature basket
- Glue gun

## Project Note

Unless otherwise stated in
instructions, use #16 tapestry
needle and worsted weight yarn
when working with 7-count plastic
canvas; use #18 tapestry needle
and sport weight yarn when working with
10-count plastic canvas.

## Cutting

**1** Cut shoppe pieces, roof and roof trim pieces, awning and awning trim pieces, chimney pieces, shutters and base from 7-count plastic canvas according to graphs (pages 166–169).

**2** Cut wagon handle from black 10-count plastic canvas according to graph (page 168), cutting away blue lines. Cut wagon wheels, grandfather clock, washboard and both signs from clear 10-count plastic canvas according to graphs (pages 167–169).

**3** From clear 10-count plastic canvas, cut one 11-hole x 7-hole piece for wagon bottom, two 11-hole x 3-hole pieces for wagon long sides and two 7-hole x 3-hole pieces for wagon short sides.

## Shoppe

**1** Stitch front, back and sides, working uncoded areas with ivory worsted weight Continental Stitches.

**2** Using dark green sport weight yarn, Backstitch and Straight Stitch flower stems and leaves; Backstitch detail on windows and doors. Work maroon worsted weight French Knots for flowers and gold metallic braid French Knots for door knobs.

**3** Overcast top edges. Using the regular Whipstitch or Binding Stitch (page 168), Whipstitch front and back to sides.

## Base & Shutters

**1** Stitch base and Overcast outside edges. Stitch and Overcast shutters, working uncoded background with maroon worsted weight Continental Stitches.

**2** Work flower stems and leaves on shutters with dark green sport

weight yarn. Work flowers with ivory worsted weight French Knots.

**3** Whipstitch front, back and sides to base with ivory and maroon worsted weight.

**4** Tack shutters to sides and back on both sides of windows.

## Roof, Awning & Chimney

**1** Stitch chimney, awning and roof pieces, reversing one awning side before stitching.

**2** Overcast bottom edges of chimney front and back, scalloped edges of trim pieces from blue dot to blue dot, and side edges of chimney opening on roof pieces from arrow to arrow.

**3** Using Binding Stitch or regular Whipstitching and Overcasting through step 5, Whipstitch top edges of roof pieces together, then Whipstitch roof trim B pieces to bottom edges of roof. Whipstitch roof trim A pieces to side edges of roof and trim B.

**4** Whipstitch awning trim to bottom edges of corresponding awning pieces. Whipstitch side edges of awning front to angled edges of awning sides, making sure to Whipstitch side edges of trim pieces together. Overcast remaining edges.

**5** Whipstitch chimney front and back to sides. Overcast top edges.

**6** Work ivory worsted weight Backstitches, Straight Stitches and French Knots on assembled roof and awning following graphs.

**7** Whipstitch bottom edges of chimney sides to bottom edges of chimney opening on roof. Tack bottom edges of chimney front and back to roof.

**8** Using dark green yarn, tack top edge of awning to front where indicated with blue line, then tack

awning sides in place. Place roof on shoppe and tack in place.

**9** Using gold metallic braid, hang liberty bell inside front left corner of awning.

## Signs

**1** Work uncoded background on both signs with ivory sport weight Continental Stitches; Overcast with maroon sport weight. Embroider letters when background stitching is completed.

**2** Using maroon sport weight throughout, tack open sign to front on right side of door; tack shoppe sign above awning.

## Clock & Washboard

**1** Stitch and Overcast both pieces following graphs, working uncoded area on grandfather clock with ivory sport weight Continental Stitches.

**2** When Background stitching and Overcasting are completed, work embroidery with black floss and gold metallic braid.

**3** Using brown, attach clock to front on left side of door.

**4** Glue washboard to base and to right front corner of shoppe.

## Wagon

**1** Stitch and Overcast wheels. Using maroon sport weight yarn through step 2, Continental Stitch sides and bottom.

**2** Whipstitch short sides to long sides, then Whipstitch sides to bottom. Center one end of handle on top front edge of wagon and Overcast over both thicknesses to attach handle; then continue Overcasting remaining top edges.

**3** Attach wheels to wagon with black yarn.

**4** Glue wagon to front left corner of base.

## Finishing

**1** Tie a short length of maroon sport weight yarn in a bow and glue to flocked teddy bear for bow tie.

**2** Glue teddy bear to base between clock and door. Glue miniature basket to base beside washboard. #

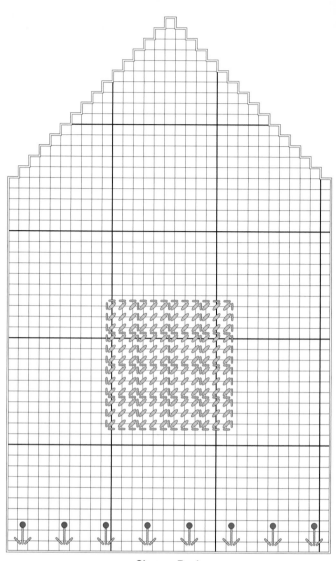

**Shoppe Back**
31 holes x 50 holes
Cut 1 from 7-count
Stitch with worsted weight yarn

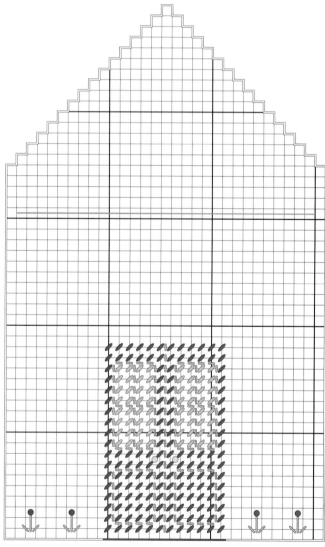

**Shoppe Front**
31 holes x 50 holes
Cut 1 from 7-count
Stitch with worsted weight yarn

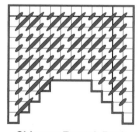

**Chimney Front & Back**
12 holes x 11 holes
Cut 2 from 7-count
Stitch with worsted weight yarn

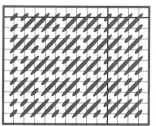

**Chimney Side**
14 holes x 11 holes
Cut 2 from 7-count
Stitch with worsted weight yarn

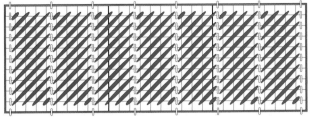

**Shoppe Awning Front**
29 holes x 10 holes
Cut 1 from 7-count
Stitch with worsted weight yarn

**Shoppe Awning Side**
7 holes x 7 holes
Cut 2, reverse 1, from 7-count
Stitch with worsted weight yarn

**Awning Side Trim**
7 holes x 3 holes
Cut 2 from 7-count
Stitch with worsted weight yarn

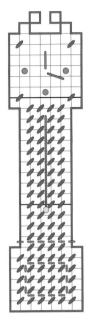

**Grandfather Clock**
7 holes x 28 holes
Cut 1 from clear 10-count
Stitch with sport weight yarn

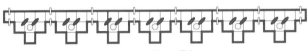

**Awning Front Trim**
29 holes x 3 holes
Cut 1 from 7-count
Stitch with worsted weight yarn

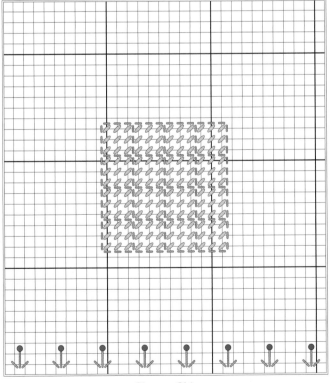

**Shoppe Side**
31 holes x 35 holes
Cut 2 from 7-count
Stitch with worsted weight yarn

| COLOR KEY | |
|---|---|
| **Worsted Weight Yarn** | **Yards** |
| ■ Dark green | 70 |
| ▨ Light gray | 50 |
| ■ Maroon | 35 |
| Uncoded areas on shoppe front, back and sides are ivory Continental Stitches | 90 |
| Uncoded areas on shutters are maroon Continental Stitches | |
| ⁄ Ivory Backstitch and Overcasting | |
| ○ Ivory French Knot | |
| ● Maroon French Knot | |
| **Sport Weight Yarn** | |
| Maroon | 10 |
| ■ Brown | 4 |
| ■ Black | 2 |
| ▨ Tan | 2 |
| □ Light gray | 1 |
| Uncoded areas on clock and signs are ivory Continental Stitches | 6 |
| ⁄ Maroon Overcasting | |
| ⁄ Dark green Backstitch and Straight Stitch | 12 |
| **6-Strand Embroidery Floss** | |
| ⁄ Black Backstitch and Straight Stitch | 4 |
| ● Black French Knot | |
| **Medium Metallic Braid** | |
| ○ Gold French Knot | 1 |

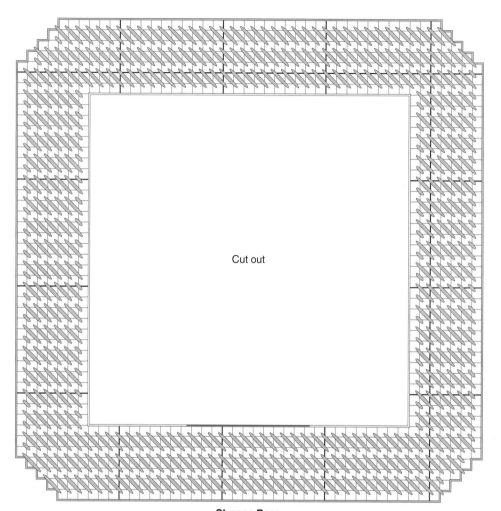

Cut out

**Shoppe Base**
45 holes x 45 holes
Cut 1 from 7-count
Stitch with worsted weight yarn

**Wagon Wheel**
4 holes x 4 holes
Cut 4 from clear 10-count
Stitch with sport weight yarn

**Wagon Handle**
5 holes x 2 holes
Cut 1 from black 10-count,
cutting away blue lines
Do not stitch

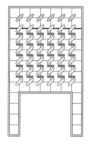

**Washboard**
7 holes x 12 holes
Cut 1 from clear 10-count
Stitch with sport weight yarn

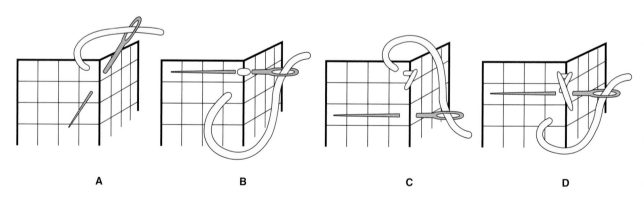

| A | B | C | D |

**Binding Stitch**

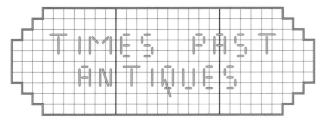

**Shoppe Sign**
29 holes x 10 holes
Cut 1 from clear 10-count
Stitch with sport weight yarn

**Roof Trim A**
29 holes x 29 holes
Cut 2 from 7-count
Stitch with worsted weight yarn

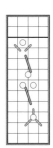

**Shoppe Shutter**
4 holes x 12 holes
Cut 6 from 7-count
Stitch with worsted weight yarn

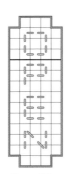

**Open Sign**
5 holes x 14 holes
Cut 1 from clear 10-count
Stitch with sport weight yarn

**Roof Trim B**
37 holes x 3 holes
Cut 2 from 7-count
Stitch with worsted weight yarn

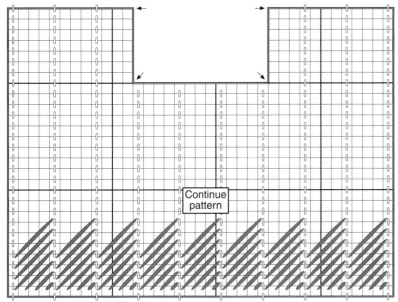

Continue pattern

**Shoppe Roof**
37 holes x 27 holes
Cut 2 from 7-count
Stitch with worsted weight yarn

| COLOR KEY | |
|---|---|
| **Worsted Weight Yarn** | **Yards** |
| ■ Dark green | 70 |
| ☐ Light gray | 50 |
| ■ Maroon | 35 |
| Uncoded areas on shoppe front, back and sides are ivory Continental Stitches | 90 |
| Uncoded areas on shutters are maroon Continental Stitches | |
| ⁄ Ivory Backstitch and Overcasting | |
| ○ Ivory French Knot | |
| ● Maroon French Knot | |
| **Sport Weight Yarn** | |
| Maroon | 10 |
| ■ Brown | 4 |
| ■ Black | 2 |
| ☐ Tan | 2 |
| ☐ Light gray | 1 |
| Uncoded areas on clock and signs are ivory Continental Stitches | 6 |
| ⁄ Maroon Overcasting | |
| ⁄ Dark green Backstitch and Straight Stitch | 12 |
| **6-Strand Embroidery Floss** | |
| ⁄ Black Backstitch and Straight Stitch | 4 |
| ● Black French Knot | |
| **Medium Metallic Braid** | |
| ○ Gold French Knot | 1 |

# Garden Globe Potpourri Ball

Design by Judi Kauffman

Hang this elegant ball in a window where spring breezes will blow the scent of potpourri through your home.

## Skill Level • Advanced

### Finished Size

3-inches in diameter, excluding hanger and embellishments

### Materials

- 3-inch Uniek QuickShape plastic canvas globe
- Kreinik ⅛-Inch Ribbon as listed in color key
- #16 tapestry needle
- 2 (6-petal) white ribbon flowers with pearl centers
- ½ yard 1½-inch-wide pink and green shaded wire-edged ribbon (sample used sheer ribbon)
- Seam sealant
- Craft glue

### Instructions

**1** Stitch top and bottom following graphs (page 172), keeping ribbon flat and smooth while stitching. Begin and end stitches as necessary by making a knot on wrong side. Make sure to align halves where they connect before stitching in order to have a mirrored pattern.

**2** Fill halves with potpourri. To connect halves, align top and bottom, then Whipstitch together with star pink Cross Stitches, working over eight bars for three Cross Stitches and nine bars for four Cross Stitches. Make small knot for last stitch on outside; secure with seam sealant.

**3** Using photo as a guide through step 4, tie wire-edged ribbon in a bow. Cut a 10-inch length from gold confetti ribbon; tie ends together in a knot to form a loop for hanging.

**4** At top of ball, glue bow, hanging loop and ribbon flowers, placing flowers back to back and knot of hanging loop at bottom. Allow to dry. #

# Diamonds & Roses Tissue Box Cover

Design by Janelle Giese

Soft blooming roses and gemlike diamond motifs
combine with Cross Stitches to create this beautiful beaded tissue topper!

## Skill Level • Beginner

### Finished Size

Fits boutique-style tissue box

## Materials

- 1½ sheets 7-count plastic canvas
- Uniek Needloft plastic canvas yarn as listed in color key
- Kreinik Heavy (#32) Braid as listed in color key
- #16 tapestry needle
- 80 Mill Hill Products ice #92010 large bugle beads from Gay Bowles Sales
- White carpet thread
- Fine sewing needle

## Instructions

**1** Cut and stitch plastic canvas according to graphs (page 172).

**2** Stitch pieces following graphs, working uncoded areas between lilac Cross Stitches with baby blue Continental Stitches.

**3** For sides, Straight Stitch star pink metallic braid accents above lavender petals where indicated. Use lavender to work a horizontal Straight Stitch over lavender and star pink petal stitches, then work a star pink stitch above lavender Straight Stitch.

**4** Attach ice bugle beads with Backstitches where indicated using carpet thread.

**5** For top piece, Straight Stitch star pink accents next to lavender petals where indicated. Use lavender and star pink to work horizontal and vertical Straight Stitches over lavender and star pink petal stitches.

**6** Work star pink Straight Stitches next to moss leaves on each flower where indicated.

**7** Overcast inside edges on top and bottom edges of sides. Using Cross Stitches, Whipstitch sides together, then Whipstitch sides to top. #

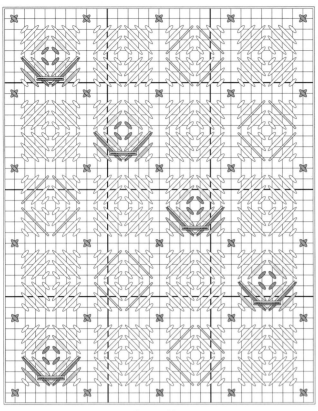

**Cover Side**
30 holes x 37 holes
Cut 4

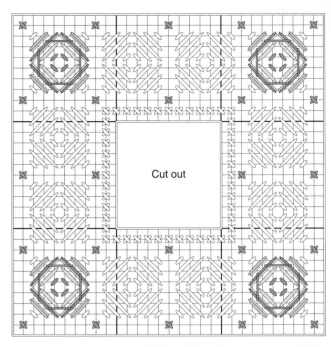

Cut out

**Cover Side**
30 holes x 30 holes
Cut 1

**COLOR KEY**

| Plastic Canvas Yarn | Yards |
|---|---|
| ■ Lavender #05 | 7 |
| ▢ Pink #07 | 5 |
| ▢ Moss #25 | 3 |
| ☐ White #41 | 52 |
| ■ Lilac #45 | 8 |
| Uncoded areas are baby blue #36 Continental Stitches | 26 |
| ∕ Lavender #05 Straight Stitch | |

**Heavy (#32) Braid**

| | |
|---|---|
| ∕ Star pink #092 Straight Stitch | 4 |
| ∕ Attach bugle bead | |

Color numbers given are for Uniek Needloft plastic canvas yarn and Kreinik (#32) Heavy Braid.

**Garden Globe Potpourri Ball continued from page 170**

**COLOR KEY**

| 1/8-Inch Ribbon | Yards |
|---|---|
| ■ Fuchsia #024 | 7 |
| ☐ Confetti gold #045 | 7 |
| ▢ Star pink #092 | 9 |

Color numbers given are for Kreinik 1/8-inch Ribbon.

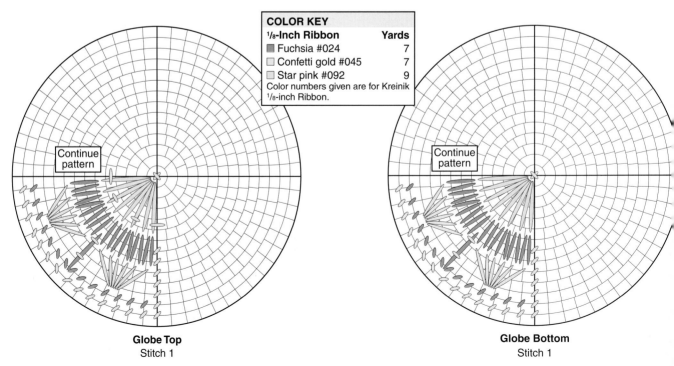

**Globe Top**
Stitch 1

Continue pattern

Continue pattern

**Globe Bottom**
Stitch 1

# Special Thanks

We would like to acknowledge and thank the following designers whose original work has been published in this collection. We appreciate and value their creativity and dedication to designing quality plastic canvas projects!

**Debra Arch**
Sunshine Quilt Block Organizer

**Angie Arickx**
Americana Picnic
Basket Tissue Topper,
Black Elegance Frame & Box Set,
Color Blocks Tissue Topper,
Mock-Woven Basket Set,
Pretty Posies Bathroom Set,
Watermelon Pinwheel Table Set

**Vicki Blizzard**
Fancy Flower Fridgies

**Janna Britton**
Diamond Princess Photo Frame,
Keepsake Egg,
Spring Flowers Stocking

**Ronda Bryce**
Stars & Stripes Wallet Key Chain,
Tasseled Bookmarks,
Tropical Toucan

**Pam Bull**
Ojos de Dios Wall Hanging

**Celia Lange Designs**
Soup-er Day Recipe Sign

**Judy Collishaw**
Shadow & Lace Roses,
Summer Shades Eyeglasses Case,
Sweet Millie Mouse Air Freshener Cover

**Mary T. Cosgrove**
A Bit of Ireland Treasure Box

**Nancy Dorman**
Antique Shoppe Tissue Topper

**Patricia Everson**
Red Barn Birdhouse

**Janelle Giese**
Bargello Kitty,
Diamonds & Roses Tissue Box Cover,
Floral Impressions Coaster Set,
Frosty Family Wall Hanging,
Frosty Starcatcher,
Noah's Sampler,
Quilted Home,
Victorian Cracker Cottage,
Victorian Elegance Key Minder

**Joan Green**
Blue Willow Tissue Box

**Judi Kauffman**
Garden Globe Potpourri Ball

**Kristine Loffredo**
Americana Nesting Boxes,
Labyrinth Tissue Holder,
Little Miss Ladybug & Frog Prince,
Secret Dreams Journal Cover,
Sparkle Butterflies

**Alida Macor**
Create-Your-Own Patchwork,
Flowers on the Square &
Good Luck Rainbow,
Midnight Blossoms Keepsake Box,
Daughter's Lament,
Pastel Frame Mini Mirror,
Variations on a Theme

**Maryanne Moreck**
Delicate Sachet Set,
Holly Angel,
Native American Patchwork Box,
Pretty Posies Eyeglasses Case

**Cynthia Roberts**
Birthday Pin

**Kimberly A. Suber**
Aquamarine & Pearls Photo Frame,
Gingham Scallops Coasters

**Ruby Thacker**
Coaster Ensemble,
Golden Crocuses Boxes,
Golden Vines Picture Frame

**Kathy Wirth**
Amish Quilt Tissue Box Cover,
Elegant Monogram
Checkbook Cover,
Frisky Felines Tissue Box Cover,
Happy Dreams Tissue Box Cover,
Interwoven Doily,
Leaf Study Coasters,
Potpourri Box,
Vase of Flowers Bookmark

**Linda Wyszynski**
Sewing Notions Box

# Stitch Guide

Use the following diagrams to expand your plastic canvas stitching skills. For each diagram, bring needle up through canvas at the red number one and go back down through the canvas at the red number two. The second stitch is numbered in green. Always bring needle up through the canvas at odd numbers and take it back down through the canvas at the even numbers.

## Background Stitches

The following stitches are used for filling in large areas of canvas. The Continental Stitch is the most commonly used stitch. Other stitches, such as the Condensed Mosaic and Scotch Stitch, fill in large areas of canvas more quickly than the Continental Stitch because their stitches cover a larger area of canvas.

**Continental Stitch**

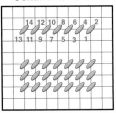

**Condensed Mosaic**

**Alternating Continental**

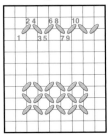

**Cross Stitch**

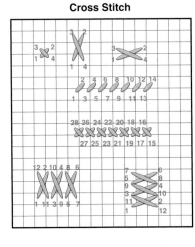

**Long Stitch**

**Slanted Gobelin**

**Scotch Stitch**

## Embroidery Stitches

These stitches are worked on top of a stitched area to add detail to the project. Embroidery stitches are usually worked with one strand of yarn, several strands of pearl cotton or several strands of embroidery floss.

**Lattice Stitch**

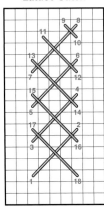

**Chain Stitch**

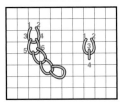

**Straight Stitch**

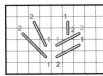

**Fly Stitch**

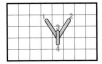

**Couching**

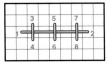

**Running Stitch**

**Backstitch**

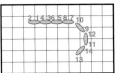

# Embroidery Stitches

### French Knot

Bring needle up through canvas.

Wrap yarn around needle 1 to 3 times, depending on desired size of knot; take needle back through canvas through same hole.

### Lazy Daisy

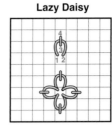

Bring yarn needle up through canvas, then back down in same hole, leaving a small loop.

Then, bring needle up inside loop; take needle back down through canvas on other side of loop.

### Loop Stitch or Turkey Loop Stitch

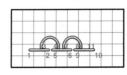

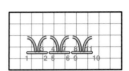

The top diagram shows this stitch left intact. This is an effective stitch for giving a project dimensional hair. The bottom diagram demonstrates the cut loop stitch. Because each stitch is anchored, cutting it will not cause the stitches to come out. A group of cut loop stitches gives a fluffy, soft look and feel to your project.

# Specialty Stitches

The following stitches can be worked either on top of a previously stitched area or directly onto the canvas. Like the embroidery stitches, these too add wonderful detail and give your stitching additional interest and texture.

### Diamond Eyelet

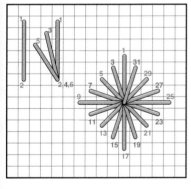

For each stitch, bring needle up at odd numbers and down through canvas at center hole.

### Smyrna Cross

### Satin Stitches

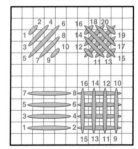

This stitch gives a "padded" look to your work.

# Finishing Stitches

### Overcast/Whipstitch

Overcasting and Whipstitching are used to finish the outer edges of the canvas. Overcasting is done to finish one edge at a time. Whipstitch is used to stitch two or more pieces of canvas together along an edge. For both Overcasting and Whipstitching, work one stitch in each hole along straight edges and inside corners, and two or three stitches in outside corners.

### Lark's Head Knot

The Lark's Head Knot is used for a fringe edge or for attaching a hanging loop.

# Buyer's Guide

When looking for a specific material, first check your local craft and retail stores. If you are unable to locate a product locally, contact the manufacturers listed below for the closest retail source in your area or a mail-order source.

**The Beadery**
P.O. Box 178
Hope Valley, RI 02832
(401) 539-2432
www.thebeadery.com

**Bucilla**
1 Oak Ridge Rd.
Humboldt Industrial Park
Hazelton, PA 18201-9764
(800) 842-4197
www.bucilla.com

**Coats & Clark**
Consumer Service
P.O. Box 12229
Greenville, SC 29612-0229
(800) 648-1479
www.coatsandclark.com

**Creative Beginnings**
P.O. Box 1330
Morro Bay, CA 93442
(800) 367-1739
www.creativebeginnings.com

**DMC Corp.**
Hackensack Ave. Bldg. 10A
South Kearny, NJ 07032-4688
(800) 275-4117
www.dmc-usa.com

**Elmore-Pisgah Inc.**
204 Oak St.
Spindale, NC 28160
(800) 633-7829
www.elmore-pisgah.com

**Gay Bowles Sales Inc.**
P.O. Box 1060
Janesville, WI 53547
(800) 447-1332
www.millhill.com

**Kreinik Mfg. Co. Inc.**
3106 Lord Baltimore Dr. #101
Baltimore, MD 21244-2871
(800) 537-2166
www.kreinik.com

**Kunin Felt Co./Foss Mfg. Co. Inc.**
P.O. Box 5000
Hampton, NH 03842-5000
(603) 929-6100
www.kuninfelt.com

**Plaid Enterprises Inc.**
3225 Westech Dr.
Norcross, GA 30092
(800) 842-4197
www.plaidonline.com

**Rainbow Gallery**
7412 Fulton Ave., #5
North Hollywood, CA 91605-4126
(818) 982-4496
www.rainbowgallery.com

**Rhode Island Textile Co.**
P.O. Box 999
Pawtucket, RI 02862
(800) 556-6488
www.ritextile.com

**Therm O Web**
770 Glenn Ave.
Wheeling, IL 60090
(847) 520-5200
www.thermoweb.com

**Uniek**
Mail-order source:
**Annie's Attic**
1 Annie Ln.
Big Sandy, TX 75755
(800) 582-6643
www.anniesattic.com